Date Due

APR 15 1983		
MAY 3 1 1988		
MAR 0 1 2012		

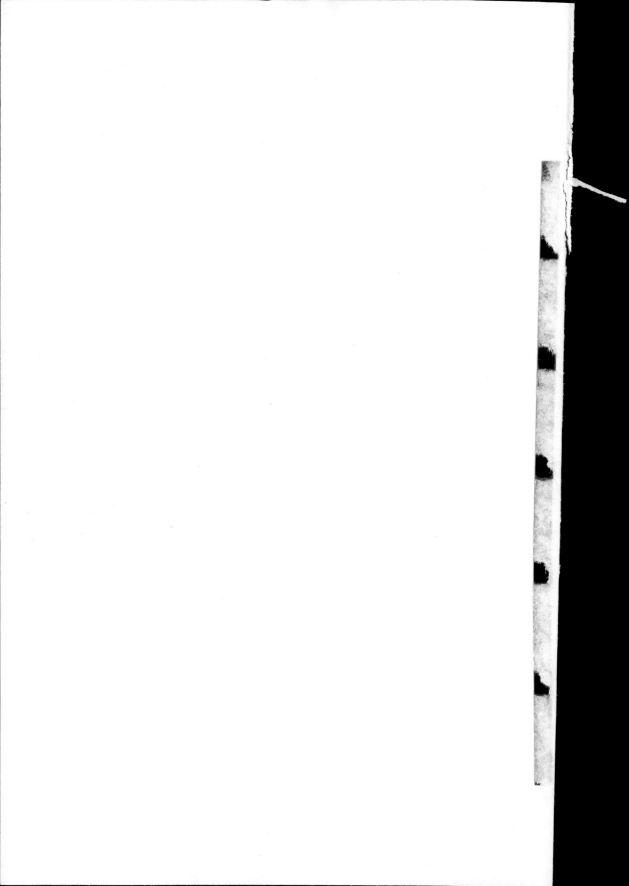

A PREFACE TO
GRANTS ECONOMICS

PRAEGER STUDIES IN GRANTS ECONOMICS

General Editors:
Kenneth E. Boulding
Janos Horvath

A PREFACE TO
GRANTS ECONOMICS

The Economy of Love and Fear

Kenneth E. Boulding

PRAEGER SPECIAL STUDIES • PRAEGER SCIENTIFIC

Library of Congress Cataloging in Publication Data

Boulding, Kenneth Ewart, 1910–
   A preface to grants economics.

   (Praeger studies in grants economics)
   Includes index.
   1. Grants-in-aid. 2. Economics. I. Title.
II. Title: Grants economics. III. Series.
HJ200.B68   336.1'85   81-10718
ISBN 0-03-059661-0   AACR2

Published in 1981 by Praeger Publishers
CBS Educational and Professional Publishing
A Division of CBS, Inc.
521 Fifth Avenue, New York, New York 10175 U.S.A.

© 1981 by Praeger Publishers

123456789   145   987654321

Printed in the United States of America

Introduction

This little volume is the product of a long process of thought and interaction. As a young man I was a very pure economist. My purity was destroyed by going to Iowa State College in 1943 to become a labor economist. In this process I discovered the other social sciences, and though I later left the field of labor economics, I came to see the social system as a total pattern—of which economics is only a part. This fortuitous discovery led me into general systems, and in 1954 I became active in a group that was later called the Society for General Systems Research. At the same time I was active in founding the *Journal of Conflict Resolution*, still very much alive, and the Center for Conflict Resolution at the University of Michigan, now alas defunct. My combined interest in conflict theory and general systems produced *Conflict and Defense* (New York: Harper & Row) in 1962. This book was an attempt to develop something like a general theory of conflict and conflict management, drawing very heavily, it must be confessed, on the techniques of economics.

A critical question, however, remained unsolved: What elements of the social system make some conflicts creative and fruitful and others destructive and damaging to all parties? I concluded that the main problem lay in what I have come to call the integrative system—that is, the aspect of society that deals with status, identity, community, legitimacy, loyalty, benevolence, and so on, and, of course, the appropriate opposites. This approach could almost be defined as the study of "how things come to hold together and how they fall apart." Still an economist, I naturally asked myself how the famous measuring rod of money might be used to measure the relationships of the integrative system; this question set me onto the idea of the grant, or the one-way transfer, as a measure of integrative relationship. If *A* gives *B* something and *B* does not give *A* anything in the way of an economic good, then there must be some kind of integrative relationship between them. I concluded that studying the grants matrix—that is, who gives what to whom—could throw a great deal of light on the clusterings of the integrative structure. I received a small grant from the Ford Foundation to study grants and was unusually fortunate in finding an associate in this work, Dr. Martin Pfaff, who with his brilliant wife, Dr. Anita Pfaff, both now of the University of Augsburg in Bavaria, took the ball that I was fumbling with and carried it much further than I ever thought it would go.

With Dr. Janos Horvath, now the John W. Arbuckle Professor of Economics at Butler University, Indianapolis, Indiana, we formed the Association for the Study of the Grants Economy. This association, formed in 1968, though very modestly financed and run mainly by personal grants of time and energy, has prospered. It has about 500 members all over the world. It presents papers and panels at a large number of professional conventions, as befits its interdisciplinary interests. The association holds an international seminar every four years in Augsburg, Bavaria. The 1978 seminar celebrated the tenth anniversary of the association; the occasion was marked by the publication of the Tenth Anniversary Brochure, edited by Martin Pfaff and published by the Center for the Study of the Grants Economy at the International Institute for Empirical Social Economics (INIFES), 8901 Augsburg-Leitershofen, Haldenweg 23, Federal Republic of Germany.

I was not very far into the study of the grants economy before it became clear that grants, or one-way transfers, come out of two different motivations and two different subsystems within the larger social framework. On the one hand, grants are products of integrative relationships and the integrative system; on the other hand, they are also products of threat and the threat system. There are two kinds of grants; gifts, arising out of "love," and tribute, arising out of "fear"—hence the subtitle of this work. Furthermore, there are many cases in which the motivations are clearly mixed, as, for instance, in the tax system, so that the grants economy cannot be separated clearly into an integrative sector and a threat sector.

It became clear that the grants economy is a segment of the social system with a good deal of independence and unity, no matter what the motivation and no matter whether the grants arise primarily out of integrative structures or out of threat structures. Furthermore, it became evident that a large part of the study of grants falls within the boundaries of economics. It deals with transfers of economic goods, and it is dominated by the phenomenon of scarcity in that the total volume of grants in any particular segment of society is limited by the innumerable forces in society that do in fact limit the amount of grants. Thus, if A gets a grant, probably some unfortunate B will not.

So I returned to moderately pure economics by the back door and discovered that there is an interesting and complex web of relationships between the grants economy and the exchange economy, which greatly expands the common image of economics as the study of how society is organized by exchange. The existing intellectual framework of economics can easily be expanded to incorporate the grants economy. Further, the grants economy is an important link between economics and the other social sciences. At the integrative level it moves toward sociology; at the threat level it moves toward political science.

The concept of a grants economy has far more than academic significance. Indeed, it is at the heart of the great controversy in the world today between centrally planned economies and market-type economies, and between radical egalitarian societies and what might be called business societies, both capitalist and communist. I have made a few comments on this controversy in Chapter 5, but the problem clearly needs more extensive study. The car of justice, shaky and broken down as it usually is, nevertheless must ride on the road of the dynamic process of the grants economy if it is to get anywhere. This alone is justification for studying these matters. Without some notion of how the grants economy develops, the rhetoric of social justice remains wind and bellyaching.

The present volume is a substantial revision of the volume entitled *The Economy of Love and Fear*, published by Wadsworth in 1973. Chapter 3, which is the core of the work, has been completely rewritten and represents, I believe, a somewhat novel approach to the problem of the total economy, which goes somewhat beyond the macroeconomic approach of the 1973 volume.

The reaction of the economics profession to the idea that grants economics should be a regular subdiscipline within the larger field was one of not always polite skepticism. In the early 1970s the general view in the profession seemed to be covered by the old remark that what was good was not new and what was new was not good. Now, however, the mood seems to have changed; the International Economic Association, which received our early presentations with sharp disapproval, even organized a seminar on grants economics in Cambridge, England, in 1979. One hopes, therefore, that the idea that one-way transfers are as much a part of economics as two-way transfers may not seem as shocking as it once was.

A large number of people have helped in this enterprise, more than could possibly be thanked individually. I must thank the Ford Foundation, whose grants helped to produce this work. Many of the ideas of this book have come out of long discussions with Drs. Martin and Anita Pfaff and with Dr. Janos Horvath. Without them, indeed, the Association for the Study of the Grants Economy would not exist. I have also learned much from the many participants in the meetings and conferences of the Association for the Study of the Grants Economy and from those who have contributed to its publications, especially Dr. Thomas Wilson. Without their stimulation I suspect this volume would never have been written. I must also thank the publishers, Wadsworth, who published the first series on grants economics, and Praeger, who is publishing the present series.

Their help and cooperation have played a most important part in this whole enterprise. I must also thank my cousins, Edwin and Muriel Wells of West Wickham, Kent, England, in whose hospitable home the first draft of this work was written. Finally, I must thank my secretary, Vivian Wilson, who is a collaborator in all my intellectual enterprises, and Valerie Ball and Judy Fukuhara, who so skillfully transcribed and typed this manuscript.

Contents

A PREFACE TO
GRANTS ECONOMICS

1

The Concept
of the Grant

THE NATURE AND DIMENSIONS OF GRANTS

A beggar approaches me, and I give him a coin. My son is going through college, and I pay for his education and upkeep. I write a check for charity. I receive a bequest from a deceased relative. A foundation makes me a grant for a research project. I pay my taxes to the government. These familiar transactions have one thing in common—they involve one-way transfers of economic goods. A one-way transfer, which is a change in ownership of economic goods from a donor to a recipient, differs from an exchange, which is a two-way transfer of economic goods. When I go into the store and buy a shirt, the storekeeper transfers the shirt to me, and I transfer the money to him. When a government department purchases an automobile, it receives the automobile from the seller, and it pays the seller the purchase price in money. An employer hires a person to do a job, and the person performs services that are valuable to the employer and receives a wage in return. All of these two-way transactions fall under the general heading of "exchange."

On the whole economists, as well as other social scientists, have concentrated heavily on the concept of exchange in describing social relationships and the organization of society, and they have regarded the one-way transfer, or grant, as exceptional and apart from the general framework of economic or social theory. This focus is unfortunate, for not only is the one-way transfer a significant element in social life, but it is an element whose importance has been growing rapidly in the twentieth century. Today, for instance, according to various possible definitions, we could say that from about 20 to almost 50 percent of the U.S. economy is organized by grants rather than by exchange.[1] The grants that are made by

1

and to governments are traditionally included in the field of public finance. However, they are similar in many ways to private transfers and cannot be analyzed readily under the usual formulations of exchange. Thus, it is time that the one-way transfer be taken into the main body of social science as a respectable and well-established phenomenon, for no social theory can be complete without it. I use the term *grant* as a generic name for the one-way transfer, as it seems to have the broadest connotation of any name that might be used.

It is not always easy to distinguish grants from exchanges. Some things that look like grants—such as the support of children by parents in traditional societies—are, in fact, more like deferred exchanges. Indeed, it has been argued that all grants are exchanges of some kind. Marcel Mauss, for example, comes close to this position in his pioneering work on the gift.[2] It is true that when I give a coin to a beggar, it can be said that something is passing from him to me in return in the form of status, recognition, or some subtle psychological transfer. These noncommodity transfers, however, real and valuable as they may be, are not recognized by accountants; and accounting practice, limited and arbitrary as it may be, at least gives a clear practical distinction between grants and exchange in terms of redistribution of net worth.[3] By accounting conventions, an exchange is a rearrangement of assets of equal values among owners, but the total net worths of the parties are not changed. For example, if A buys $100 worth of wheat from B, A has $100 worth of wheat more and $100 of money less, B has $100 of money more and $100 worth of wheat less, but the net worths of both the parties are unchanged. On the other hand, if A makes a grant of $100 to B, then A's net worth is diminished by $100 and B's net worth is increased by $100. Although it can be complained that accounting measures do not cover all phenomena of social or motivational significance, this distinction is still fundamental. Insofar as accounting measures do generally cover economic goods, or exchangeables, the net worth criterion can be effectively used to distinguish a grant as any two-party relationship in which an exchangeable passes one way but no exchangeable passes the other way, even though there may be non-exchangeables passing between the two parties.

THE RANGE OF GRANTS CONCEPTS

What we have here, very common in the real world, is a spectrum of concepts within which the definitions and classifications are a matter of literary convenience. There is a grants-exchange continuum. At one end there is pure exchange in which there are no grants elements. At the moment of pure exchange there is a redistribution of assets between two parties, where each party gives up exactly what the other gets. The items are valued in such a way that there is no change in the net worth of either party. Stock and bond market transactions or purchases in a supermarket come fairly close to this, though there are always certain underlying grant elements in terms of trust, legal recourse, recontract, and so on, if any one of the parties feels legitimately dissatisfied. Toward the middle of the spectrum we have reciprocity—reciprocal grants that are not subject to contract but to informal understanding. Such arrangements almost certainly have preceded contractual exchange in human history. These arrangements tend to be nonquantitative, informal, but they may be very important, and violations of these implicit understandings may result in eventual sanctions. The whole role of sanctions, that is, underlying threat in exchange relationships, is a very interesting one that has been little explored. At the far end of the scale there is the pure grant—redistribution of net worth with no expectation of any reciprocal return. I must confess that I feel a good deal of this when I pay my income taxes!

There is also another dimension that underlies the grants-exchange distinction, which is the spectrum with economic goods at one end and noneconomic goods at the other. Definitions here also are by no means clear. Money, commodities, anything we buy in the store, stocks, bonds, and so on, are clearly economic goods. Respect, status, affection, prestige, courtesy, and so on, are clearly noneconomic goods. There is, however, a fairly hazy area in the middle. What, for instance, is the status of an honorary or an earned degree, a title, an elected office, an invitation to a dinner party? Is a wife or a husband an economic good? The answer may depend very much on the nature of the culture.

Within the grants economy itself there are other dimensions that, again, have something of the attributes of spectra. The organizational environment of grants is one such dimension. At one end of this we have grants that are part of a budget. In an organization a budget is a plan for the allocation of funds to different departments. Such allocations fall under the definition of a grant in that they increase the net worth of the department and diminish the net worth of the central allocating agency. Within any organization a department receives its income not from the direct sale of services or goods but from a central budget or accounting office. Budget grants are characteristic of all organizations, whether public, private, capitalist, socialist, religious, educational, and so on. The ability to make decisions about internal transfers, indeed, is one of the principal marks of status in a hierarchy, another phenomenon that no organization can escape. The higher a person stands in an organizational hierarchy, the more he is a boss and the less he is bossed and the more internal grants he has the power to control. Bosses make budget grants; the bossed receive them.

At the other end of this spectrum we would have, say, the gift of a private individual for the relief of suffering in an area victimized by disaster in another country. Here there is no discernible organization that unites the donor and the recipients, no hierarchical relationship by which the donor can give conditional grants. Even in this case, however, while there is no organization, there must be something of a sense of community, even if the community is as vague as the common humanity that unites the donor and the recipients in a sense of pity.

Between these two extremes we have the family, which is a loose, informal organization but which nevertheless may have something like a budget. We can think of the transfers that a parent makes to a child as internal transfers within the departments of the larger organization of the family. The transfers are made because the higher members of the hierarchy (parents) have something like a budget in which grants are made to children, in the best interest of the larger organization, which is the family itself. The family, of course, is an organization in constant flux as its members are born, leave home, marry, age, die, and so on. But even the theory of the firm might be in better shape if it were recognized that the firm—and all organizations—is also in a constant state of flux. Somewhere toward the nonbudget end of the scale is the relief organization or the foundation that allocates grants out of its budget, not, however, to its own departments but to exterior persons or organizations.

Another dimension within the grants concept that is very important is concerned with the motivations for one-way transfers. Here we have gifts at one end of the scale and tribute at the other end. The pure gift is an expression of benevolence and involves an identification on the part of the giver or donor who parts with the gift with the welfare of the recipient who gets it. As a grant in the accounting sense, a gift represents a transfer of net worth from the donor to the recipient. A little further down the scale, the gift may begin to look like a budget grant if the donor regards the assets of the recipient as part of his own asset structure. The gift is more like the rearrangement of assets among parts of a single organization than it is a true transfer. As we have seen, grants within the family may fall into this category. Further down the scale, we get the gift that is conditional on the recipient's doing something of which the donor approves, even though the donor may not himself directly benefit by this activity. Research grants by foundations have something of this character.

At the opposite pole from the gift (a grant made out of benevolence) is tribute—that is, a grant made out of fear and under threat. A threat is a statement of the form, "You do something that I want or I will do something you do not want." The extreme form of tribute is the bandit or holdup man who says, "Your money or your life." You give him your money, which is a grant in the accounting sense of the word, since it clearly diminishes your net worth and increases his. There is no benevolence, though; such transactions are much more likely to produce malevolence, even if it does not exist already. The transaction looks superficially like an exchange: I give the bandit my money; he gives me my life. The resemblance is only superficial, however, because the absence of a negative commodity—that is, not taking my life—is by no means the same as a positive commodity. In the algebra of the world of exchangeables, two negatives do not make a positive.

Few grants rest clearly at one or the other end of the spectrum; in almost all grants we find a certain mixture of the two motivations, opposite as they are. Consider, for example, the tax system. We pay taxes to governments or other taxing authorities partly under threat. If we do not pay them, our property will be confiscated or we will go to jail or experience something else disagreeable. In this sense the government is like the bandit. However, to a surprising extent we also consent to pay taxes because we identify with the objectives of the taxing authority, whether it be a school district, a city, or a national state. If the taxing authority loses its legitimacy (that is, its capacity to command acceptance) in the eyes of the taxpayer, it becomes more and more like a bandit; the cost of collecting taxes rises, tax resistance appears, and in extreme cases the whole power of the taxing authority may collapse.

These mixtures of love and fear are distressingly untidy, but they seem to characterize a great deal of human behavior. Even within the family, parents support the children not only because they love them but also because they are afraid of what the neighbors might say, or they fear for their reputation, or they even fear the heavy hand of the political authority coming down with legal sanctions for child neglect. Even in the case of the intraorganizational grant or budget payment, we find something of the same mixture. A university supports its economics department partly because the decision makers feel that the economics department is an essential part of a good university—so they support it partly out of love—but also partly out of fear that if they abolish the economics department, the reputation of the university will suffer.

MOTIVATION BY UTILITY MAXIMIZATION

Economists tend to approach the problem of motivation through the concept of utility, which is a hypothetical measure of the well-being of a person or group, particularly as expressed in their individual preferences. Utility is that which goes up when a change produces a situation that is preferred to the previous situation in the mind of some evaluator. The only motivation of the individual then is to maximize utility as the individual perceives it, which does not amount to very much more than saying that everybody does what is thought to be best at the time. In the pure economic theory of exchange it is supposed that utility does not rise proportionately with the quantity of an asset but rises at a diminishing rate. The rate of its rise is marginal utility, so that the previous principle is often called the law of diminishing marginal utility. As exchange proceeds, the marginal utility of the asset that is being acquired (x) continues to diminish, whereas the marginal utility of the asset that is being given up (y) continues to increase until the point comes where the two are equal. At this point the trader will refuse to exchange any further, because the next amount of x that would be given up is not worth, in his own estimation, the amount of y that would be received. In a free exchange either party may exercise this veto, depending on which one first reaches the point at which further exchange is no longer advantageous. If exchange is pushed beyond this point, the total utility of the vetoing party is diminishing, though that of the other party may still be increasing.

This principle, although very formalistic, nevertheless is useful in relating preference structures to behavior, and it seems to be curiously neglected by psychologists. The principle can easily be expanded, however, to include the gift made under benevolence. All we have to suppose is that the perception of one party, A, of the welfare of the other, B, is a variable in A's utility function such that when A perceives that B is better off, A's utility rises. This would be the definition of A's benevolence. Here, again, we can suppose that utility is maximized at the point where one party vetoes any further expansion of the gift. We usually think of the donor, A, as the vetoer who will stop expanding the gift at the point where the loss in utility through the diminution of A's assets is exactly balanced by the gain due to A's perception of the increase of the welfare of the recipient, B. An even stronger parallel with exchange is that it is conceivable for the recipient, B, to veto any further expansion of the gift. A benevolent recipient, B, may veto an expansion of the gift at the point where B perceives that the benefit to B due to an increase in the gift is offset by the decline in B's utility as a result of contemplating the loss of the gift to A. If the recipient does not want the gift, and if it involves noneconomic costs in subservience, unwanted gratitude, or dependency, so that the gift does not add much to the recipient's utility, this point can come fairly soon. Professors have been known to turn down grants that have been offered to them. The conditions of the gift also enter into this, especially if the condition of the gift is to do something that the recipient does not really want to do in comparison with other things that might be done.

Utility theory can also be applied to tribute, that is, to a grant made out of fear. I give the bandit my money because the diminution in utility that this represents is less than the diminution that is represented by the expected value of my loss of life. Whereas exchange is a positive-sum game in terms of utility, tribute is likely to be a negative-sum game if the utility gained by the bandit minus the utility cost of making the threat, which in some cases may be quite considerable, is more than offset by the utility lost to the victim. In threat situations also, therefore, utility theory is a perfectly reasonable description of motivation. Here, again, everybody does what he thinks is best at the time. With a longer time perspective, of course, what is thought to be best at the time is sometimes regretted in a later context, but that is another matter.

Over the course of human history the relative proportions of gift to tribute or love to fear in the grants system undoubtedly change. What determines this change and even the direction it takes is not easy to discover. It is at least a possible hypothesis that, over the course of time, the threat element diminishes and the integrative or gift element in grants increases.

Without some kind of integrative structure in the way of a widespread acceptance of the legitimacy of authority, and at least a minimum of benevolence toward those in the same community, it is very hard to organize a threat system beyond a very limited range. The bandit can organize a temporary social system with a considerable grants element in it. However, if he wants to do this every week, he must either become a tax collector or a rent collector or fill some other economic role that is recognized and legitimate. It is to the subtle dynamics of the integrative system—that set of social relations involving status, identity, community, legitimacy, loyalty, love, and trust—that we have to look if we are to understand the growth and structure of the grants economy. In some degree, however, this operates by the legitimation of threat, for instance, in a tax system. Without some form of legitimated threat it is very hard to provide public goods and to avoid "tragedies of the commons,"[4] by which a behavior that is rational and utility maximizing for each member of a community has the result of making everybody worse off.

USES OF THE GRANTS CONCEPT:
CHARITY, PUBLIC FINANCE, BUDGETS

It is not enough to produce a set of definitions and a taxonomy, or system of classification. Those of us who have been concerned with developing the theory of the grants economy have been accused by some economists of simply inventing a new set of terms and concepts for an old and familiar body of theory. The proof of any set of concepts, and of any taxonomy, is, of course, in the using, and the reader will have to judge for himself by the end of this book whether these concepts are in fact useful.

At this point we can at least ask ourselves what kinds of problems that could not be solved so easily in conventional terms might be more readily solved with the aid of the concepts of grants economics.

The most obvious problems that seem to require a grants concept as their basic framework are connected with the phenomenon of charity. Whether it be a casual gift to a beggar, the establishment or conduct of a foundation, the support of religious, medical, educational, and research enterprises, or even government redistributions of income, this phenomenon is extremely hard to explain using the conventional theory of exchange, and indeed it plays no part in the conventional economic theory of welfare economics, the study of the extent to which economists can say whether one state of affairs is better or worse (economically) than another. Economics has a theory of the firm, as it exists in an exchange economy; it has no theory of a foundation and no very good theory of a government as an economic organization, partly because of its neglect of the grants concept.

The grants concept may also be significant in the areas of public finance and the provision of public goods. Public finance, which is primarily the study of government receipts and expenditures, is a classical area of economics that has had a respectable history and a great deal of empirical study from the days of Adam Smith. Nevertheless, it has never had a really satisfactory theoretical base—I suspect because it has been studied by economists trained primarily in the theory of exchange who have tried to force public finance into that mold on the assumption that if taxes are paid, the taxpayer must receive something for them. The grants concept liberates public finance from its enslavement to the concept of exchange and enables us to perceive the whole system as a system of related one-way transfers rather than as a system of exchange.

Closely related to the problem of public finance is the problem of public goods, which has aroused a good deal of interest among economists in recent years. A public good is one that cannot be appropriated and (if it is provided at all in a community) can be enjoyed by any member of the community, whether in fact he contributes to its provision or does not. If public goods are to be provided at all, there must be something like a grants economy. Individuals must transfer resources from their private accounts to the public authority without receiving any specific benefit; or to look at the matter from the other side, they can enjoy goods that are provided by other people without having to pay for them or make any sacrifices for them. Public goods will not be provided at all, therefore, if there is not something like a grants economy, whether public or private, whether gifts, tribute, or some mixture of the two. Thus, the theory of public goods cannot be separated from the theory of the grants economy.

Another area in which the concept of the grants economy is important is the theory of organization. We have already noted that internal transfers of resources from one part of an organization[5] to another, and from one level of hierarchy to another, is a crucial element in the functioning of organizations of all sizes, from the family right through to the socialist state. Grants, therefore, are a particularly significant element in what might be called political economy—that is, the processes by which roles are created and things get done by nonmarket machinery, whether in corporatins, churches, departments of defense, or international organizations. Without the grants concept any kind of organization would be incomprehensible.

Finally, the grants concept throws a great deal of light on some of the political controversies of our times, particularly the socialist controversy. The core of the socialist controversy is a dispute about the legitimacy of market organizations versus grants organizations. Capitalism relies more on the market, especially on capital markets, to organize society and perform its essential functions. The socialist countries rely much more on a political economy of budget grants. Nevertheless, the grants concept points up the fact that there is a large overlap between the socialist and capitalist worlds and that the organization of any large capitalist corporation is in fact very similar to that of a socialist country, both of them having to rely extensively on a system of budget grants and direct allocations in their internal organization. Although it may be too much to expect the grants concept to resolve the ongoing dispute about the relative merits of socialist and capitalist economies, we can certainly expect the study of the grants economy to provide insight into the issues and to pinpoint many of the real questions in dispute.

PARALLEL FUNCTIONS OF GRANTS AND EXCHANGE: ALLOCATION, DISTRIBUTION, AND DEVELOPMENT

There are other considerations that point up the autonomy and independence of the grants sector of the economy and the consequent necessity for independent study of this sector. If we look at the traditional functions of the exchange sector of society—that is, of markets (the organization involved in buying and selling) and the price structure (the set of prices or ratios at which things are exchanged)—we find that every one of its major functions is paralleled in the grants sector. One major function of the exchange sector is the allocation of resources among different occupations and industries. This determination of how large each segment of the economy should be is accomplished by the price-profit mechanism. This mechanism works in such a way that if any segment of the economy is too large in relation to the demand for its product, the price of its product will have to be too low for that segment to be normally profitable. Thus, resources formerly used in producing the product will flow into more profitable segments of the economy. Conversely, if any segment is too small, the price of its product will be too high; it will be unusually profitable, and resources will flow into it. Hence, if we define equilibrium as a specified state, position, or range of positions of a system, divergence from which produces activity designed to correct this divergence, then we can say that a pure exchange system will develop an equilibrium of distribution of resources among different occupations and industries. For given stages of technology this condition will be fairly stable, although dramatic long-run shifts need not be ruled out.

The grants sector of the economy also plays a significant role in the allocation of resources. Suppose we postulate a "resources neutral" structure of grants, in which the allocation of resources and the mix of commodities in the output of the economy do not change. If the beggar buys a cup of coffee with the coin I give him, and if because I have given him the coin I find myself unable to buy a cup of coffee, then the grant redistributes income, but it does not redistribute resources. If people were not taxed to provide a public education system, they might use their income to purchase in the free market an educational system of the same kind. The very improbable nature of these illustrations, however, suggests that a grants system that is neutral in terms of the distribution of resources is extremely unlikely. Furthermore, it is usually the explicit objective of a set of one-way transfers to reallocate resources in a direction that the grantor finds desirable. Thus, intraorganization grants (budgets) are used by the central authority of any organization to reallocate resources within the organization, for instance, toward or away from sales or maintenance or this or that department. Grants within the family, likewise, usually have the objective of changing the activity of the recipient, as when a parent pays for his child to go to college. Grants from foundations are usually devised to push the recipients into activities that they might not have performed otherwise. Similarly, foreign aid grants are usually tied to some development program with the objective of making the recipient do something that he would not have done under other conditions. If a grants system were to be neutral in the distribution of resources, therefore, the grants would have to be carefully planned with neutrality as a goal. However, there is virtually no motivation to plan grants in this way; indeed all the motiviation is in the other direction.

A very interesting question is whether it makes sense to postulate an equilibrium in the allocation of resources in a combined system of exchange and grants. On the whole economists have regarded grants as a somewhat arbitrary distortion of the equilibrium produced by the unfettered operation of an exchange economy. This view seems very unrealistic.

It is by no means implausible to suppose that the political demands and the community preferences that provide a complex mixture of benevolence, malevolence, and demand for public goods in the grants economy could not also produce something like an equilibrium in the allocation of resources. Presumably all activity originates from some sense of divergence between an ideal and a perceived real value of some variable or condition, so that the equilibrium concept is just as reasonable to apply to the grants economy as it is to the exchange economy. Thus, if the market demand for education seems to provide an educational industry that is widely recognized in a politically conscious way as too small, the grants machinery will come into play to expand it, through charity or through taxation and public expenditures. And, of course, these grants force a decline in other industries, which will release resources into education.

A particularly interesting segment of society, the size of which is closely related to the overall grants economy, is crime. If we think of crime as an industry that under pure market conditions (that is, in the absence of public organization) has a strong tendency to be too large, we can visualize the police and other efforts to diminish crime as an enterprise existing mainly in the grants sector of the economy, concerned with the diminution of an industry regarded as undesirable. The crime industry itself also involves substantial illegitimate redistributions of assets, the effect of which is not well understood.

The second great function of the exchange sector of society is the distribution of income—that is, the determination of how much of the total product each person gets. The income of any person depends first on the total of his assets, including his own mind and body, and then on the prices that the market system places on the services of these assets. The distribution of income that results from the undisturbed operation of the exchange sector, however, is frequently regarded as politically or morally unacceptable by society, and hence there is intervention through both the private and the public grants economy to change the distribution of income toward something regarded as more desirable—*desirable* usually meaning more equal. Here again, we see the grants economy supplementing, or perhaps correcting, the results of the exchange economy.

Just as we can conceive a grants system that is neutral in the distribution of resources, so we can conceive a grants system that is neutral in the distribution of income or, more generally, the distribution of welfare (although this phenomenon seems even less likely than the former, as it would involve robbing Peter to pay Peter). Any society, indeed, with no grants economy or a distribution-neutral grants economy would soon cease to exist, as its children would starve to death.

In what might be called the radical egalitarian societies, such as Cuba and the People's Republic of China under Mao Zedung, the political demand for a distribution of income that diverges from distribution produced by exchange is so strong that the exchange economy itself is disrupted and severe misallocations of resources may ensue. On the other hand, in the absence of an adequate system of redistribution through grants, the exchange economy, as it does in some Latin American countries, may easily produce a distribution of income that is so unequal as to be both politically unstable and a great handicap to development.

Development, measured as genuine growth in per capita real income, may be regarded as a third function of both the exchange economy and the grants economy, as it combines both aspects of allocation of resources and distribution of income. In part this is a problem in the allocation of resources to what might be called the developmental industry, that is, that segment of activity that is peculiarly significant from the point of view of increasing wealth, power, or social integration in the future. There is a very widespread belief that the exchange economy, while it will allocate some resources to development, will allocate an amount that is too low to be politically acceptable and that, hence, the grants economy must again intervene to expand this particular segment of economic and social activity. The distribution of income, however, is also relevant to the developmental process. This process can easily be frustrated if its fruits are not widely distributed and can equally be frustrated if its fruits are distributed too widely and too soon. In all these three cases the problem of the right proportions and the interaction of the exchange economy and the grants economy is perhaps the most important question in political economics, and it underlies, as we saw earlier, the whole socialist controversy.

THE IMPLICIT GRANTS ECONOMY

A significant aspect of the relationship between the exchange and the grants economy is the concept of an implicit grants economy, which comes about as a result of political distortions of the price structure or, more generally, of the structure of exchange. Almost anything a government does in the way of regulations, prohibitions, quotas, quantitative restrictions, licensing, and so on, will alter the relative price structure,[6] which will in turn lead to either temporary or permanent shifts in the distribution of income and assets. In other words, any such government participation in the economy will make some people richer and other people poorer, constituting an implicit grant from those who are made poorer to those who are made richer. If, for instance, some person or group of persons is given a monopoly of some commodity, the price of that commodity will rise, and there will be an implicit grant from all the people who purchase it to those who produce or control it. A tariff, likewise, will have complex redistributional effects, injuring consumers and perhaps benefiting producers of the country imposing the tariff, injuring producers and perhaps benefiting consumers in the other countries. These implicit grants are enormously complex and very hard to discover in most practical cases. The elusive quality of such grants has political importance because it means that political conflict rests to a very large extent on a universal ignorance of consequences, as the people who are benefited by any particular act or policy are rarely those who have struggled for it, and that the people who are injured are rarely those who opposed it. This might almost be called the law of political irony—that what you do to help people hurts them, and what you do to hurt people helps them.

Another aspect of implicit grants concerns the distribution of the benefits of any development. When the per capita real income of the society increases, who gets the increase, and who sacrificed in order to get it? Part of the increase may be regarded as a grant from nature; part of it is a result of sacrifices made in the past. Development, however, benefits many people who made no sacrifices for it. A thorough study of the implicit grants economy over time would be extremely difficult, but it clearly represents a very important aspect of society. It would involve things like rates of return on investment; the amount and distribution of capital losses and of windfall capital gains; the rise of the proportion of national income going to labor, which has been so striking in developing societies in the last hundred years; and the whole question, so beloved of classical economists, of the rise or fall in economic rents. This is a range of important questions almost frightening in its complexity, but they are questions that can hardly even be raised unless there is some concept of a grants economy.

While the general concept of an implicit grants economy is clearly relevant and significant, defining it is difficult since it requires setting up a no-grants price system as a norm, divergences from which would be an implicit grants economy. We do have something approximating such a norm in the concept of the structure of alternative costs—that is, the amount of commodity A that must be given up in order to produce one more unit of commodity B. If the resources released by not producing one of Adam Smith's[7] famous beavers could then be utilized to produce two deer, there would be a strong tendency for two deer to exchange for one beaver in the marketplace, because if market prices were not in this ratio, working in the high-price industry would be more profitable than the other and resources would flow into it out of the other. This would lower the high price and raise the low price until the alternative cost ratio was again established. We might then have some confidence in supposing that if by government regulation or other circumstances the relative price of beaver were kept higher than this and the relative price of deer lower, the resulting shifts in the distribution of income would represent an implicit grant from the deer producers to the beaver producers. The measurement of these implicit grants, however, is an empirical and statistical problem of great difficulty. I shall develop these concepts more fully as this volume proceeds.

THE ROLE AND EVALUATION OF GRANTS IN THE DYNAMICS OF SOCIETY

One of the odd things about the grants economy concept is that it seems to arouse great anxiety and hostility among many more traditional economists. I admit I am a little puzzled by this, as grants economics seems to me a very natural and obvious extension of the existing frame of thought in economics and in the social sciences generally. Indeed, the whole concept seems so obvious that it is hard to believe that it has not been developed before. The very hostility that the concept arouses, however, suggests that there is enough novelty in it at least to upset those whose economics is confined very strictly to the concepts of the exchange economy. Naturally, the only proof of the pudding is in the eating, and I hope that this presentation will demonstrate the usefulness of viewing the concept as a natural evolution of the existing conceptual framework in economics and in the other social sciences.

In recent years we have seen a great deal of interest, particularly among political scientists and sociologists, in the theoretical framework of the exchange economy, and there have been some successful attempts to apply this framework to the larger field of social and political relations. I have sometimes called this movement economics imperialism because there are times when it looks like an attempt on the part of economics to take over all the other social sciences. It would be disastrous, however, if the social sciences unified themselves solely around the concept of exchange—even as generalized by George Homans[8] in sociological exchange or as by David Easton[9] and by Warren Ilchman and Norman Uphoff[10] in political exchange—without recognizing that exchange, even in its most general form, is only one of the social organizers and that the grant as an organizer becomes even more important as we move away from economics toward sociology and political science.

The dynamics of the grants economy—the processes by which it grows, declines, or changes its form, sources, or recipients—are so complex as to involve the dynamics of the whole society, and specific dynamic models are probably not much use at this point. Nevertheless, we can see some patterns and at least outline some hypothetical relations. Thus, the perceived efficiency of grants is likely to be an important variable.

Efficiency is the ratio of perceived benefit to the recipient to the perceived cost for the donor. Thus, if by sacrificing $1 I perceive that somebody else is $4 better off, my perception of the efficiency of the grant is 4. If I perceive that by sacrificing $1 somebody else is only $0.50 better off, my perceived efficiency is 0.5. Clearly, the greater the perceived efficiency, the more likely we are to expand our total of grants, and we are also likely to expand grants in the direction in which we perceive the greatest efficiency. The willingness to make gifts, indeed, depends on two main factors: the perception of the efficiency of the grant and the degree of identification with the welfare of the recipient, that is, the degree of benevolence toward him. These processes, however, by which we learn malevolence or benevolence and derive our perceptions of efficiency are complex and mysterious and cannot be reduced to any simple model.

Our willingness to pay tribute also rests on our perception of its efficiency and on the degree of malevolence toward the recipient. If we perceive the tribute as efficient, that is, as benefiting the recipient whom we hate, we will be less willing to pay it than if we perceive it as not benefiting the hated recipient or as benefiting a recipient that we do not hate so much. We will also be more willing to pay tribute the more we perceive to be the cost and credibility of the threat.

The most important and most difficult problem is how to evaluate both grants and exchange in all their complex and ramified structures according to what is desirable for society. The problem has two very closely interrelated aspects. One must consider first the general problem of what proportion of the activities of society should be organized by grants and what proportion by exchange. This question is the heart of the socialist controversy. The answers that will be given will then depend in large part on a further set of evaluations of the legitimacy of exchange or of grants in different situations, or even on what we interpret in fact as being exchange or being grants. Thus, capitalist economists have usually regarded interest together with profit as essentially part of the exchange economy and, on the whole, a legitimate part of it. Socialist economists, by contrast, have considered this phenomenon part of the grants economy, as representing a grant from the workers to the capitalists and an illegitimate grant at that. This disagreement is fundamental and not easy to resolve, although this difficulty may be partly due to the fact that neither party to the dispute has really had a satisfactory theory of the grants economy. Underlying all these disputes, however, is a set of questions about the deficiencies or the pathology[11] of both the exchange economy, on the one hand, and the grants economy, on the other.

The pathology of exchange is familiar—depressions, inflation, unemployment, maldistribution of income, inadequate public goods, and so on. The pathology of the grants economy is less familiar because we have not thought about it so much in these terms. Particular elements of it, however, are familiar in economic literature. For instance, there is the great discussion of the poor law in classical economics, the discussion of the distributional impacts of tariffs and taxes, the impact of the minimum wage and rent control, and so on. These questions tend to be considered in isolation, though, and have not been seen as part of a larger system. Nevertheless, they are highly relevant and will be discussed later in this volume (see Chapter 7).

Our evaluation of the relative merits and the relative proportions of grants and exchange in the total system will depend a great deal on our evaluation of the relative efficiencies and the relative proneness to pathological states of the two systems. The absence of any theoretical vision of the grants sector of the economy as a system in its own right has distorted opinion and, in some degree, has prevented the resolution of this dispute. We are highly conscious of the nature and the pathologies of the exchange economy. Because we are much less conscious of the nature and pathologies of the grants economy, the grants economy has had an unfair advantage in this dispute. It is only as we come to see the exchange economy and the grants economy as equal partners in the total social enterprise that we can properly determine the role that should be assigned to each. This volume is a modest attempt to correct the present imbalance and to assist the process of more careful and more accurate evaluations.

NOTES

1. James N. Morgan and Nancy A. Baerwaldt, of the University of Michigan, estimated the following figures (in billions of dollars) for transfer payments in the U.S. in 1970: business transfers, 3.6; government transfers, 73.9; interfamily transfers, 8.4; intrafamily transfers, 313.2. By comparison, the GNP was $976.8 billion. Private philanthropy, including foundation grants, was estimated at about $20 billion in 1972. James N. Morgan and Nancy A. Baerwaldt, "Trends in Inter-Family Transfers," in *Surveys of Consumers, 1971-72,* ed. Lewis Mandell (Ann Arbor: Survey Research Center, Institute for Social Research, University of Michigan, 1973). A more recent study suggests that these proportions are fairly stable. See "5000 American Families: Patterns of Economic Progress," ed. Greg J. Duncan and James N. Morgan, vol. 6, no. 347.366(Ann Arbor: Institute for Social Research, University of Michigan, 1978).

2. Marcel Mauss, *The Gift: Forms and Functions of Exchange in Archaic Societies* (New York: W. W. Norton, 1967).

3. The *net worth* of a person or an organization is the sum of the value of the assets minus the sum of the value of the liabilities associated with the owner of the net worth. It is a dollar value expressing somewhat inaccurately, but still meaningfully, the net value of capital owned.

4. See Garrett Hardin, "The Tragedy of the Commons," *Science* 162 (1968): 1243-48.

5. An organization could almost be defined as a set of roles, linked by one-way transfers of economic goods and communications. Communications are supposed to be two-way, that is, exchange, but they rarely rise above reciprocity, especially in the hierarchical structure.

6. The relative price structure is the set of ratios of exchange of all pairs of commodities. Thus, if bread is $0.10 a pound and butter is $0.80 a pound, the relative price is eight pounds of bread per pound of butter. If after an inflation bread were $1 a pound and butter were $8 a pound, the relative price would be unchanged.

7. Adam Smith, *The Wealth of Nations* (New York: Random House, Modern Library Edition), Book 1, chap. 6, p 47. "In that early and rude state of society which precedes both the accumulation of stock and the appropriation of land, the proportion between the quantities of labour necessary for acquiring different objects seems to be the only circumstance which can afford any rule for exchanging them for one another. If among a nation of hunters, for example, it usually costs twice the labour to kill a beaver which it does to kill a deer, one beaver should naturally exchange for or be worth two deers. It is natural that what is usually the produce of two days' or two hours' labour, should be worth double of what is usually the produce of one day's or one hour's labour."

8. George Caspar Homans, *Social Behavior: Its Elementary Forms* (New York: Harcourt Brace Jovanovich, 1961).

9. David Easton, *A Systems Analysis of Political Life* (New York: John Wiley & Sons, 1965).

10. Warren F. Ilchman and Norman Thomas Uphoff, *The Political Economy of Change* (Berkeley: University of California Press, 1969).

11. Pathology is the study of ill health and can easily be extended to the study of the ill health of society—that is, conditions that are almost universally recognized to be bad.

2

The Micro Theory of Grants and Granting Behavior

THE TWO-PARTY RELATIONSHIP

A grant is always a relationship between two or more parties. In the simple two-party relationship it involves the grantor or donor, on the one hand, and the recipient, on the other. Thus, a grant involves at least two decisions—a decision[1] on the part of the donor to make a grant and a decision on the part of the recipient to receive it. The decision of the donor may seem to be the more significant of the two, but the decision of the recipient is by no means insignificant. There may be elements of threat in the recipient's decision to receive, just as these elements may take part in the decision of the grantor to give. It is not always unreasonable to be unwilling to receive a gift horse without looking it in the mouth. Grants can also be initiated by the recipient's asking or applying for them. Therefore, if we are to perceive the special significance of the grant in the spectrum of human relationships and behavior, we must first look at the general pattern of these relationships.

Figure 2.1 illustrates a general form of the two-party relationship. Here we have two parties, A and B, which may be either persons or social organizations. A gives up something, x_a, which he perceives as sending x_a to B. When x_a arrives at B, however, it may be something else, x_b. Similarly, B sends out y_b, and A receives y_a. These x's and y's may be commodities, such as wheat or money; they may also represent communications, information, threats, promises, affirmations, persuasions, and so on. In simple commodity exchange we generally assume that what physically leaves one party is the same as what reaches the other, that is, $x_a = x_b$ and $y_b = y_a$. Thus, A may transfer 100 bushels of wheat to B, and B will transfer at the same time $400 of money to A. However, the significance, or utility, of

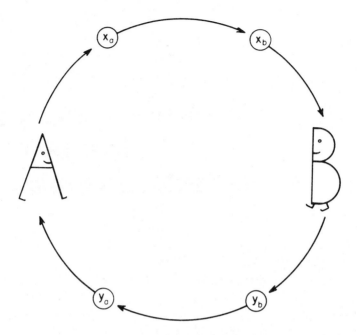

Figure 2.1. Simple Exchange

the exchangeables is different for the two parties. In the classical theory of exchange it is assumed that uncoerced exchange will not take place at all unless both parties benefit—that is, unless what *A* gives up is worth less to him subjectively than what he receives, and what *B* gives up is, likewise, worth less subjectively than what he receives. Therefore, in our simple case of the sale of wheat, the seller values the money more than the wheat and the buyer values the wheat more than the money, even though the physical quantities transferred do not change in the act of transfer.

Even in the simplest two-party relations there are more than two things transferred. Thus, the x_a, x_b, y_a, and y_b of Figure 2.1 really represent packages or combinations of things. In the case of simple exchange, then, it is not merely commodities that are transferred but also information, communications, or messages. If I pass a store window and see a shirt with a price tag on it that I would like to buy, I have perceived a message from the storekeeper saying, "I am willing to give you this shirt, if you will give me this amount of money." When I go into the store, I have to communicate with the storekeeper before he will bring the shirt out of the window so that the transaction can take place. It is almost impossible to think of any relationship among people in which communication does not play some part.

In communication, of course, the possibility that what leaves one party will not be what the other party receives—that is, that x_a will not be the same as x_b, and that y_b will not be the same as y_a—is very strong. A's communication x_a comes out of A's image of the world. When it arrives as x_b at B, even if it has not been transformed or distorted in the process of transmission, it has to pass into B's image of the world to achieve significance, and the significance it has for B may be different from what it originally had for A. Such distorted perceptions are a common source of misunderstanding in communication. The situation is further complicated in that x_a depends on A's image of the significance that the receipt of it will have for B, and A's image of the significance for B may be very different from B's image of its significance.

In many forms, even in commodity exchange, the difference between x_a and x_b and between y_b and y_a may be of great significance. We see this, for instance, in the labor market, where the exchange of labor for money is much more complex than, shall we say, the exchange of money for stocks and bonds in the financial market. Thus, if A is the employer and B is the worker in Figure 2.1, x_a represents the money wages the employer pays out, the significance to him depending on the alternative uses of the money, for example, to improve his capital equipment or expand his loans. What the worker receives, x_b, even though it may represent the same number of dollars, has a very different significance for the worker. For him it represents in real terms the consumer goods he can buy with it. The y_b, which is what the worker gives up, is so many hours a day, the significance of which depends on the alternative uses of his time, either in other jobs, in self-employment, or in leisure. The y_a that the employer receives acquires its significance from the product of the work, especially the marginal product, or the additional product produced by the additional work.

It is not surprising, then, that the labor market is the focus of so much conflict, waste, and anxiety and that it creates a sociological environment that is totally different from that of the stock market or the wheat market. Even the organizations surrounding the labor market—trade unions and employees' associations, conciliators, mediators, government agencies, and so on—cannot be explained only in terms of the simple economics of monopoly power, or attempts at monopoly power, but they have to be explained largely in terms of the extreme communication difficulties involved in this type of relationship. Because of the different life experiences of workers and employers, it is very hard for either of them to put themselves in the other's place and see the world from the other's point of view. Consequently, communications are almost invariably distorted—A's image of B's world is very different from B's image of his own world, and B's image of A's world is, likewise, very different from A's image of it. This situation can breed an enormous amount of misunderstanding and unnecessary conflict. We should not assume, of course, that misunderstanding always increases conflict. It is probable that if people knew what the real world was like, they would perceive real conflicts of interest that they may not perceive now because of misunderstanding.

To make our picture of the two-party relationship more complete, we can express it as in Figure 2.2 where the solid lines $x_a x_b$ and $y_b y_a$ represent transfers of some sort of material objects—commodities, money, or services—and the dotted lines $x'_a x'_b$ and $y'_b y'_a$ represent flows of information and communication. The grant is, then, the special case in which one of the commodity flows is zero; for example, in Figure 2.3, y_b and y_a are zero, and we are left with only the other commodity flow and the information and communication flows.

TERMS OF TRADE AS A MOTIVATOR

The terms of trade of the two parties is a very significant quantity in the two-party relationship. For party A in Figure 2.1, this quantity is y_a/x_a—that is, how much he takes in per unit of what he gives out. A rise in this number is an improvement in his terms of trade; he is getting more in for

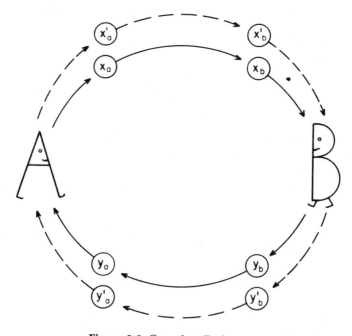

Figure 2.2 Complete Exchange

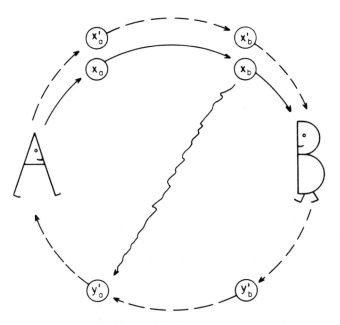

Figure 2.3 The Grant

every unit that goes out. Similarly, B's terms of trade are x_b/y_b. If now $x_a = x_b$ and $y_b = y_a$, which we generally assume in simple commodity exchange, then A's terms of trade, T_a will be the reciprocal of B's terms, T_b, or

$$T_a = \frac{1}{T_b}. \tag{2.1}$$

Thus, suppose $x_a = x_b = \$400$ and $y_b = y_a = 100$ bushels of wheat, where A is buying wheat from B at \$4 per bushel. B's terms of trade are \$4 per bushel; A's are one-fourth bushel per \$1. If the price rises, say, to \$5 per bushel, the seller's (B's) terms of trade improve, and the buyer's (A's) worsen to one-fifth bushel per \$1. Under these circumstances, of course any improvement in A's terms of trade means a worsening of B's terms of trade. This is the essence of the conflict in exchange. There is, indeed, a curious paradox about the phenomenon of simple exchange in that it involves both a conflict and a community of interest. There is community of interest on the assumption that the exchange is not coerced, for the exchange will not take place unless both parties benefit. On the other hand, there may well be a conflict of interest in the terms of the exchange—that is, in the terms of trade, or the ratio of exchange. Everybody likes to have a high price for the things that he sells and a low price for the things that he buys, so that any change in the structure of the relative prices will create some sort of redistribution of welfare, about which there may be conflict.

When we go to the general case of the two-party relationship, both the terms-of-trade concept and the conflict concept become much more complex. In Figure 2.1 if x_a is not equal to x_b and y_b is not equal to y_a, then the simple reciprocal relationship of equation 2.1 breaks down. A can improve his terms of trade without a worsening of B's, for example, if y_a rises relative to y_b. Thus, A's and B's evaluations of loss or gain in the transfer process itself are important elements. If x_b is larger than x_a and y_a is larger than y_b, we have a situation that is likely to be profitable to both parties. This, indeed, is precisely the classic theory of exchange, when x_a, y_a, x_b, and y_b are interpreted as utilities. On the other hand, we cannot rule out the case in which x_b is smaller than x_a and y_a smaller than y_b. In this case neither party gets as much as the other party gives up. This, of course, operates to restrict the area within which exchange is mutually advantageous. A classical example of this situation occurs when costs of transport or transaction costs are involved in the transfers. The elements of this situation are well worked out in the theory of international trade.[2] In the classical theory of exchange the differences in utility of the two parties act, as it were, as negative costs of transport. The x_a given up by A is perhaps something he did not want very much because he has a lot of it. This factor is transformed into a much larger x_b when it arrives at B, in terms of B's utility, because this is something that B wants a good deal, perhaps because he does not have very much of it. Similar considerations hold for the y's.

When we look at the complete exchange of Figure 2.2, the terms of trade have to be measured by each party's evaluation of the inputs and outputs. Thus, suppose that in the estimation of party A, the total value or utility to him of x_a is $x_a v_a$. The quantity v_a is then a valuation coefficient somewhat analogous to a utility price.[3] Similarly, we have valuation coefficients v_a for the output x'_a, u_a for the input y_a, u'_a for the input y'_a, and similar concepts for party B. The terms of trade T'_a for A and T'_b for B are now given by equations 2.2 and 2.3:

$$T'_a = \frac{y_a u_a + y'_a u'_a}{x_a v_a + x'_a v'_a} \tag{2.2}$$

$$T'_b = \frac{x_b v_b + x'_b v'_b}{y_b u_b + y'_b u'_b}. \tag{2.3}$$

Now, of course, it would only be under very unusual conditions that the reciprocal relationship of equation 2.1 would hold. In the special case of the grant relationship (Figure 2.3) we suppose that y_b and y_a are zero, so that equations 2.2 and 2.3 reduce to equations 2.4 and 2.5 respectively:

$$T'_a = \frac{y'_a u'_a}{x_a v_a + x'_a v'_a} \qquad (2.4)$$

$$T'_b = \frac{x_b v_b + x'_b v'_b}{y'_b u'_b} . \qquad (2.5)$$

The basic theoretical assumption in all these cases is that the two-party relationship either will not come into being at all or will break down and cease to be if the utility terms of trade of both parties T'_a and T'_b are not greater than 1.0. If T'_a were exactly equal to 1.0, party A would be indifferent to the relationship in that A would get out of it exactly the same in utility as what he put into it. If T'_a is greater than 1.0, A has a net gain in utility and gets more out of the relationship than he puts into it. If T'_a is less than 1.0, A is getting less out of the relationship than he is putting into it, and hence he will be motivated to veto the relationship (we are assuming for the moment that each party has veto power over the relationship). Just how this comes about we shall look at later. In simple exchange, where $x_a = x_b = X$ and $y_a = y_b = Y$, equations 2.2 and 2.3 reduce to equations 2.6 and 2.7, respectively:

$$T'_a = \frac{Y u_a}{X v_a} \qquad (2.6)$$

$$T'_b = \frac{X v_b}{Y u_b} . \qquad (2.7)$$

In equations 2.2 through 2.7 putting $T'_a = T'_b = 1$ gives us two equations that define a boundary in the variable space, on the one side of which the utility terms of trade of both parties are greater than 1.0 and the two-party relation is viable. This rather simplified analysis assumes a cardinally measurable utility. As every economist knows, it is nearly always possible to reformulate the problem in terms of ordinal utilities. (I have done this in "Notes on a Theory of Philanthropy"[4] in which the conventional economic apparatus of the Edgeworth box, which is usually only applied to exchange, is extended to grants, again demonstrating that the grant from one party to another is simply a special case of the two-party relation.)

Let us now look at the grant relationship of Figure 2.3 in a little more detail. As we have seen, the grant will take place if the utility terms of trade of both parties are greater than 1.0, or at least not less than 1.0. For grantor A, this means that the loss in utility from giving up x_a must be more than balanced by the total gain in utility resulting from the output x'_a and the input y'_a. Noncommodity outputs, x'_a in this case, might consist of the release of guilt or obligation. In any case, a noncommodity output, which would carry a positive utility, would help to offset the negative utility of the commodity output. A's noncommodity inputs, symbolized by y'_a, may be of many different kinds. If A is benevolent toward B, then A's perception that B's welfare has increased represents an increase in A's welfare or utility (suggested by the wavy arrow in Figure 2.3). The more benevolent A feels toward B and the more he perceives his output x_a as increasing B's welfare, the larger will be the utility value of y'_a and the more likely is the transaction to take place.

THREATS AND NEGATIVE GRANTS

As we have seen, grants are made not only out of benevolence but also in response to threat. Thus, the noncommodity input to A (y'_a) may consist of a threat from B that if A does not make the grant (x_a), B will diminish A's utility by doing him some damage. In this case, the increase in utility represented by y'_a is a "negative negative"—that is, it is the absence of a decrease in utility that would otherwise have taken place. From the point of view of individual utility accounting, though not from the point of view of society as a whole, this may be just as effective as a positive increase in utility and may be equally influential in accounting for the existence of grants.

Looking now at B's side of the relationship, x_b, B's commodity input presumably causes an increase in his utility, although this might not always be the case. That is, assuming that x_a and x_b are approximately the same thing, what A wants to give may not be at all what B wants to receive and may, in fact, have a much greater utility for A than for B. There may also be noncommodity inputs, y_b, that have negative utility—for example, if the commodity grant is accompanied by noncommodity communications suggesting B's inferiority of status or his obligations to be grateful. Since grants almost always imply a superior status of the grantor to the recipient, the implication is that a negative noncommodity input of utility will frequently go along with commodity grants. Indeed, there is often a good deal of humiliation involved in receiving somebody else's bounty. It should be noted that there are some exceptions to the rule—for instance, gifts made by subjects to their rulers, vassals to their lords, parishioners to their clergy, and so on. Such gifts are more likely to be a result of a threat system, whether spiritual or material, and in such systems the threatener tends to have superior status. Even the bandit or the holdup man at the moment of attack has something of the status of a lord, and the victim is his vassal. Status rewards may also play a significant part in y'_a, that is, A's noncommodity inputs. If the grant made to B reinforces and symbolizes A's higher status, then in a very real sense y'_b is an output of status from B and y'_a is an input of status into A. Thus, a gift to a beggar or a lift to a hitchhiker may symbolize a rise of status to the donor.

Because of this potential element of threat, we should note that malevolence, as well as benevolence, may play a significant role in the grant relationship. If A perceives that an improvement in B's status is a negative utility to A (makes him feel worse off), or if his perception of a worsening in B's status would be a positive utility to him, then we can see malevolence at work. Under these circumstances we may get a negative grant—an output from A, even in commodity terms, that is designed to diminish B's welfare rather than to increase it. This output may take the form of poison pen letters, slander, the destruction of B's property, and, in the extreme case, the taking of B's life. Negative grants, unfortunately, are still an important element in the world system, especially in the international system, where the defense industries of the various countries are mainly concerned with producing the capability of making negative grants to other countries. Negative grants, of course, are twice cursed: they are costly to the grantor, for whom they represent utilization of resources that might have been employed in the production of positive commodities; and if the intentions of the grantor are fulfilled, they are an injury to the recipient. The record of warfare shows that negative grants are by no means uncommon.

Negative grants may not always result from malevolence. They may be executed as a kind of investment by the grantor in reestablishing the credibility of his threats. Thus, he will have the expectation of getting tribute—a commodity transferred from the other party in the future. Negative grants may also be made under conditions of benevolence, as when a parent punishes a child. It may even be true that "This hurts me more than it hurts you" and that the parent is giving negative grants to the child in the expectation that the child will thereby eventually have an increase in welfare, which will then be registered as an increase in the parents' welfare.

FOUNDATIONS

Professional granting organizations—such as foundations and, to some extent, governments—present a particularly interesting problem. The decision to set up a foundation in the first place may be analyzed as a variant of the two-party relationship of Figure 2.3. If A is the donor or establisher and B is the foundation itself, it can be said that the donor transfers commodities, securities, or money from himself to the foundation. The noneconomic transfers may include an input of status and, of course, benevolence toward the foundation itself as an extension of the donor's own interests and purposes. Foundations and charitable endowments may also be set up through threat and fear—in earlier times, for instance, through the fear of hell, and in modern times, through the fear of inheritance taxes and a preference for private grants over public grants enforced through taxation. All this, however, fits fairly well into the pattern of our previous analysis.

Once the foundation is set up and a professional staff is acquired, the situation becomes different, particularly in terms of the alternative costs of the grants. When a private person makes grants for charitable purposes, the alternative cost of the grants is what he might otherwise have done with the money, such as invest it or spend it for some immediate pleasure and satisfaction in consumable goods. A foundation does not have this option. Once the commitment has been made, the funds that it has at its disposal must be granted; they cannot be used for consumption or investment, except under very unusual circumstances. A foundation, therefore, is an organization that possesses earning assets that continually provide inputs of money into the foundation's account. Beyond a certain point, however, money is a disutility to the foundation. An increase in assets, especially liquid assets, is a disutility to it, and it must reduce its net worth by making grants. Thus, a foundation is almost literally an organization that excretes money. Decision makers of foundations have to decide to whom and for what purposes grants will be given; they rarely have the option of not making grants at all, especially where the tax laws or other laws regulate their conduct.

Foundations differ from firms in that, provided that they stay within what is usually a rather broad framework of the law, there are no very clear standards by which they or anybody else can judge whether they are being successful. A profit-making institution in a market environment has a measure of its success in its rate of profit. If it continually takes losses, it will not survive; if it makes profits, there is evidence that the institution is meeting a need that can be expressed through the exchange economy— that is, it is satisfying a demand at least as well as anybody else can satisfy it. This hypothesis leaves open, of course, the ultimate social question of whether all demands are good, but at least within a certain restricted framework there is a rather clear standard of success.

Foundations have no such standards of success. No matter to whom or for what purposes a foundation makes its grants, provided that it stays within the law and manages its investments successfully, it will survive. There is very little selective process that eliminates foundations with frivolous or unproductive purposes, in the way that there is a selective process operating to eliminate firms that do not produce something for which people are willing to pay. Because the survival of the foundation does not depend on the feedback it gets from its decisions, it has less interest in obtaining this feedback. I have sometimes called this "Edsel's law." When the Ford Motor Company produced the Edsel automobile, it soon discovered that the demand was not adequate to justify its production. There was very rapid feedback, and as a result the mistake was corrected and the Edsel withdrawn. In contrast, if the Ford Foundation produced an "Edsel" in the form of grants for purposes that were not particularly socially useful or did not produce the intended results, the foundation might never know, or might only find out after a long time, and would probably not change its policies very much once it had this information. This absence of feedback from grants is a serious defect, which could easily lead into pathological states of the grants economy. This is one point at which the exchange economy, where feedback tends to be rapid, direct, and acted upon, has a certain advantage.

Foundations can say, of course, that success consists of carrying out the purposes set forth in their charters. However, these purposes are usually very vague, and the question of their social desirability remains unresolved. There are foundations, like the famous one in St. Louis, to provide covered wagons for pioneers going westward, with purposes that are now obsolete. There are also foundations whose purposes can be criticized for their low social priority, but such criticisms are rarely made and are seldom effective even when they are made.

Nevertheless, there is something like a market in grants. Where there are a large number of grantors facing a large number of potential recipients, at least an analogue of the competitive market in the exchange sector begins to appear. Something like this market exists, at least in the more developed countries, in the field of research grants. Research is widely recognized as a highly suitable activity for grant support. Scientific knowledge is a public good in that once the discovery has been made, it is available to anyone who can understand it. This does not necessarily apply, of course, to trade secrets, classified research, and patented processes, which are more of the nature of private goods; however, the principle applies extensively over the field of pure science. As it produces a public good, science almost has to be supported by the grants economy rather than through the exchange economy. What is called science policy is very largely a matter of who shall give what research grants to whom and with what strings attached.

If there is only a single grantor, such as the government or a single agency of government, we have a monopoly situation that may lead to an undesirable concentration of power in the hands of the grantor. Where there are many grantors and many grantees, a grantee who does not get a grant from one granting agency can try another one. Hence, a creative but unfashionable grantee is less at the mercy of the whims of any particular grantor and is much more likely to find somebody who will support his idea. The case against monopolies is just as strong in the grants economy as it is in the exchange economy. It has even been suggested that we might need an "antitrust act" for foundations and that there should be a legal maximum size for a particular foundation, in which case the large foundations might have to split up into a number of independent smaller ones.

Indeed, government regulation of foundations has some of the aspects of the regulation of private monopoly. Insofar as grants are very intimately related with the political system, foundations could almost be regarded as a form of private government, and it is not surprising that public government looks on them with a somewhat careful and critical eye. Government foundations, also, like the National Science Foundation, might better serve their objective if they were split up into a number of independent agencies with overlapping jurisdictions. Organizational untidiness frequently promotes, and tidiness destroys, creativity and innovation.

RECIPROCITY AND INTEGRATION

Another relationship that is not fully included in the previous scheme is reciprocity. This may look very much like exchange, as it usually involves a two-way transfer, sometimes separated by an interval of time, of commodities or exchangeables between two parties. It is different from exchange, however, in that whereas exchange is conditional ("I will give you so much of X if you will give me so much of Y") and is based essentially on the acceptance of a conditional offer, reciprocity is formally unconditional, although in practice it often tends to edge across the spectrum into exchange. Thus, reciprocity can be defined as mutual grants or a related pair of grants. That is, A gives something to B out of sheer goodness of heart and benevolence for B, and B gives something to A out of sheer goodness of heart and benevolence toward A, yet the two acts are not being formally related since neither is a formal condition of the other. Christmas presents are a good example of an activity that frequently involves reciprocity and occasionally degenerates into exchange. The unconditional nature of the operation, however, differentiates it from exchange and perhaps explains why people rarely get what they really want for Christmas.

Conditions under which it is acceptable or not acceptable to give money rather than commodity presents would make a very interesting study. The giving of a gift also conveys a message saying, in effect, "I have gone to some trouble to get you something that I think you will like." This is a message implying regard or affection, or some sort of integrative relationship. Reciprocity, even though it looks superficially like exchange, has integrative aspects that exchange does not. The fact that commercialization of Christmas is so widely deplored suggests that reciprocity has a function in building a sense of community and a more complex structure of personal relationships that pure and simple exchange is unable to perform. I would argue that even exchange requires a degree of integrative relationship among the parties before it can be legitimated, which is why exchange almost always develops originally out of reciprocity and may be regarded historically as the formalization of reciprocity.

The formalization of reciprocity into exchange takes place not only because of the greater flexibility and convenience of exchange in getting what we really want but also because it may be an escape from the status inequality implied in the grant. As we have noted, when A gives something to B, it is frequently a symbol or even a creator of higher status for A and lower status for B. When B reciprocates by giving something to A, B restores his and A's status to what they may have been before the initial gift. Exchange, almost by its very symmetry, implies equality of status. That is, in the exchange diagram of Figure 2.2 we can interchange A and B and it makes no difference in the pattern. In the grants diagram this is not so. The relationship is not symmetrical. Exchange has the same eyeball-to-eyeball quality about it that characterizes the threat-counterthreat or deterrence system ("If you do something nasty to me, I'll do something nasty to you"), although there is much less glare in the eyeballs.

The social customs and the noncommodity inputs and outputs that surround the exchange process often develop because the equality of status implied in exchange may be at variance with the inequality of status recognized elsewhere in society. This accounts for the obsequiousness of the traditional shopkeeper toward his more exalted customers. He knows perfectly well that in the exchange transaction he has the superior status—having superior knowledge—but he has to disguise this fact in order to avoid offending his customers who are under the illusion that they have the superior status. In a supermarket there is no obsequiousness and only the bare rudiments of courtesy because the equality implied in paying dollars for groceries does not have to be denied. There is little difference in status between the housewife checking her groceries out and the clerk on the other side of the counter.

A very interesting aspect of reciprocity is what might be called serial reciprocity in which a gift from A to B creates a generalized sense of obligation on the part of B. This obligation is satisfied by a gift from B not to A but to another party C, who in turn satisfies his sense of obligation to another party D, and so on around the circle, until finally perhaps a gift comes back to *A*, and the whole process is repeated. The famous "Kula ring" of the Pacific islands is perhaps an example of this phenomenon. While some commodities circulate as gifts in one direction around a group of islands, yet another group of commodities travels in the opposite direction around the same circle.

Even in modern societies, however, serial reciprocity is by no means an insignificant phenomenon. It is very important, for instance, in the relations of the generations. The debt we owe to our parents is not often repaid to them but to our children instead, who in turn pay the debt they owe us to their children, and so on, one generation to the next. There is also a certain amount of deferred exchange or simple reciprocity in the relationship between the two generations. Parents support their children with grants—at least they did before the development of pension funds and Social Security—in the expectation that in their old age their children will support them by grants. This is reciprocity over time, rather than exchange, as it involves complex integrative relationships and is not contractually formalized. Once the support of old age is contractually formalized, of course, it ceases to be reciprocity and becomes exchange. Even the Social Security system, however, has a considerable element of public reciprocity about it and usually lacks the clear contractual exchange framework of private pensions and insurance. Its payments, for instance, are constantly revised.

One of the most important aspects of the grants economy is the role it plays in the building up of integrative structures and communities—that is, groups of people who have some feelings of identification and benevolence toward each other. The dynamics of community growth are subtle and very little understood. The one-way transfer, however, plays a very significant role in the process, partly because of a phenomenon Alvin Gouldner has called the "reciprocity multiplier" in the case of serial reciprocity.[5] A gift may be a unilateral expression by the donor of identification with the recipient. The receipt of the gift frequently creates an almost unconscious sense of obligation—perhaps, as was suggested earlier, because of the status-lowering aspects of being a recipient. If this obligation is fulfilled by a return gift, we have simple reciprocity and the circuit is closed immediately without further repercussions, even though there may be a certain buildup of integrative feeling between the two parties. If it results in serial reciprocity, there may very well be a multiplier effect involving more and more people in the community building operations of gift giving, until some sort of equilibrium is reached. We can think of the process perhaps in epidemiological terms. Thus, the original gift giver becomes a source of infection of benevolence. The infection may lose its intensity as it goes through a number of receivers and subsequent givers, but under some circumstances it may increase in intensity as it triggers off previously latent benevolent feelings. The process stops when it reaches a recalcitrant character who simply absorbs a gift without feeling any obligation to retransmit it. The gifts, incidentally, need not be commodities. They may be merely communications—smiles, courtesies, hellos, small favors, and so on.

Another source of interaction between the grants economy and the integrative system arises out of what in its pathological form I have called the "sacrifice trap." A gift helps to create the identity of the giver, and a gift either to an individual or to a cause or community identifies the giver with the recipient. Once the gift has been made, however, it is very difficult to withdraw it and also very difficult for the giver to admit he was wrong. Thus, the gift builds itself into the identity of the giver; in pathological cases he can become trapped into a disadvantageous identification with the society, organization, or cause for which he has sacrificed. This principle causes people to throw good money after bad, to throw live soldiers after dead, new martyrs after old ones, and so on. It is very hard for a politician whose decisions have cost a large number of human lives to admit either to himself or to anybody that these decisions were mistaken. In order to justify them, he often has to throw more lives into the bottomless pit of sacrifice. Up to a point the principle may be a healthy one, for without the kind of commitment or identity that emerges from sacrifice, it may well be that no communities, not even the family, would really stay together. On the other hand, the principle easily becomes pathological, as we see in war and in certain excesses of religious or political devotion, or even in the family, where people sometimes create lives of utter misery for each other because each has sacrificed so much.

Exchange has no such power to create community, identity, and commitment, perhaps because it involves so little sacrifice. This, indeed, is one of the great weaknesses of capitalism, which is organized principally through exchange. It may not be able to attract through its institutions that minimum of loyalty, devotion, and affection necessary to maintain them. Joseph Schumpeter was perhaps the first economist to point this out.[6]

TWO-PARTY EXCHANGE VERSUS MULTIPARTY GRANTS

Another source of the integrative weakness of exchange is its almost exclusive confinement to two-party relationships, whereas a grant system can easily be multiparty. Although the operations of the competitive market involve many parties, each transaction in the system is between two parties. It is very rare to find an exchange transaction involving even three parties—a contract, for instance, in which A gives something to B, B gives something to C, and C gives something to A. Even the mechanisms that

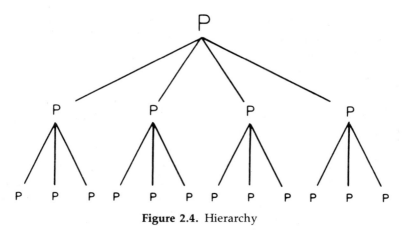

Figure 2.4. Hierarchy

create a unified market, such as arbitrage,[7] take place in individual two-party transactions. One exchange, of course, affects others in its neighborhood, so that the exchange system does maintain something like a many-parties equilibrium. This, however, is unseen, covert, and "ecological." It appears to the individual as some outside force of nature over which he has no control, and it is not surprising, therefore, that it is hard for an exchange system to command loyalties. Nobody loves a bank in the way in which he may love a country, political party, family, or church.

By contrast, grants are easily adapted to multipartied relationships. They are indeed the prime creator of large-scale organization. A hierarchy, for instance, is organized by grants rather than by exchange. With all the virtuous talk about two-way communication in organizations, it still remains true that in communication reciprocity rather than exchange is the only really obtainable ideal. An order from the boss is essentially a grant of information often accompanied by grants of commodities.

There are two major patterns of multiparty relationships. One is the hierarchy, as illustrated in Figure 2.4, the *P*'s standing for the parties. The other pattern of multiparty relationships is the group, illustrated in Figure 2.5, in which relationships go from all members to all other members. In both of these cases contractual exchange is too complex and rigid a relationship to permit much complexity in multiparty patterns. What looks like exchange is frequently reciprocity. Even in the labor market, the exchange relationship is between the individual worker and the organization. The actual organization structure, if it is hierarchical, almost has to consist of one-way transfers and one-way communications. Similarly, in the group, if exchange is relied on as the social organizer, the group will soon break up into pairs simply because it is very hard to maintain

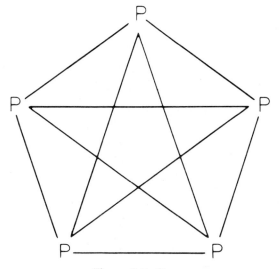

Figure 2.5. Group

exchange transactions with large numbers of people. There will indeed be reciprocity, but this, as we have seen, is something rather different from exchange. Terms of trade—what we get per unit of what we give—are still very important in a multiparty situation because if any one party finds that his terms of trade with the group, or with the organization, are poor, he will tend to leave.

Nevertheless, the terms of trade are determined in a system of reciprocity rather than in an exchange system, which is one reason perhaps why it is often difficult in these cases to correct unsatisfactory terms of trade, even when it is in the interest of the parties to do so. Thus, a man quits a company, leaves a church, or even divorces his wife because he feels that he is giving too much and getting too little. If the transactions were of simple exchange, the terms of trade perhaps could be renegotiated. Where the transactions involve reciprocity, however, negotiation and bargaining are almost ruled out by definition, and one has to rely on spontaneous changes in the flow of one-way transfers, which may be very difficult to achieve consciously. Some modern organization theorists have argued that the pathologies and inefficiencies of hierarchy could be corrected by developing exchange simulations in the middle of organizations. Whether this can really be done, however, is open to grave doubt, simply because of the sheer difficulty of organizing multiparty relationships through contract.

LABOR GRANTS

Another very significant aspect of the grants economy, which has also been neglected by economists, is the labor grant, or the voluntary provision of personal services without charge. This covers a very large area of social life and quantitatively it may be the largest single element in the grants economy. I know of no aggregate estimates of its overall magnitude. It is not always easy to tell where volunteer labor ends and leisure-time activities begin. Again, there is a wide spectrum of activity, and it is not particularly important where the actual dividing lines are drawn. There is a broad distinction between volunteer action or labor grants, which is unpaid activity designed to benefit somebody else, and leisure-time activity, which is designed primarily to benefit the person performing it. There is a great overlap, however. If a father takes his children camping, he is acting on his own behalf as well as theirs, and a great deal of the satisfaction of leisure-time activity consists in some sort of reciprocity, as in the playing of games. Being a golf partner, for instance, is a service to the opponent, who might conceivably have to pay somebody to play golf with him, as well as a leisure-time activity on the part of the person involved.

The theory of volunteer action is not very different from that of grants as a whole, just as the theory of labor supply is a special case of the theory of exchange. The motivation for a labor grant, like that of any other, may be fourfold. There may be personal satisfaction in simply performing the operation, a motivation that is likely to be more significant in a labor grant than in the grant of a commodity or money, simply because the activity itself may be interesting and significant to the performer and thus preferable to mere idleness and boredom. Even the founder of a foundation may get more personal satisfaction out of serving on its board than he would have done by idly spending the money on trivial pleasures. Another motivation we have already examined is benevolence—that is, identification with the welfare of the party benefiting from the labor grant. In this sense giving service is not very different from giving money, especially if it involves a sacrifice of earnings on the part of the giver and an increase in welfare on the part of the recipient. Like all grants, labor grants will be made if the perceived utility terms of trade are greater than 1.0—that is, if the utility derived from the activity itself, plus the contemplation of increased benefits to others with whom the actor identifies and is benevolent toward, exceeds the utility cost involved in the sacrifice of alternative uses of time and their product. The total amount of voluntary labor supplied, therefore, will be that at which an extra hour will bring in less to the supplier, in terms of additional satisfaction either in the activity itself or in the contemplation of its benefits to others, than it costs him in terms of disagreeableness of the activity and contemplation of alternative uses of the time. There will be more volunteer labor, therefore, first, the more pleasurable the activity is in itself, second, the more it is perceived as being effective in increasing the welfare of others, third, the greater the rate of benevolence, and fourth, the less the value of the alternative uses of time.

There is a certain parallel to tribute involved in labor grants, such as the taxation in kind that is involved in a compulsory draft or conscription, insofar as a draft forces people into occupations that they otherwise would not be in, at wages below what would otherwise attract them. The difference between the wage that would attract them and the wage actually paid is an implicit tax and, hence, again, can be properly regarded as part of the grants economy. There have been attempts to estimate the tax involved in the draft, paid by draftees in these terms in the United States.[8] While any exact measurement is impossible, the order of magnitude certainly ran into billions. Forced labor of any kind, the corvée of medieval France, the so-called slave labor camps of the Soviet Union, and prison labor in the chain gang in Georgia are examples of this kind of tribute labor. Compulsory education is another example. In the case of minors it could be argued that this use of threats is in the interest of benevolence and that we force children into compulsory education because they are not able at this stage to assess the advantages and disadvantages of being a student. It is hard to deny the theoretical validity of this argument, even though one may be skeptical about its application in particular cases.

An extremely interesting application of the principle of voluntary action was studied by R.M. Titmuss[9] of the London School of Economics in regard to blood donors. In the United Kingdom the blood supply for medical purposes is almost entirely voluntary. In the United States and the Soviet Union it is largely in the exchange system, and human blood is mainly a marketable commodity. Titmuss documents with great skill the consequences of these two different policies, particularly for the quality of the blood supplied, which tends to deteriorate under conditions of the market, following a kind of generalized Gresham's Law[10]—that in the absence of differentiation for quality, bad blood drives out the good.

A very interesting question in the area of social policy issues is the nature of the adjustment when there is danger that the voluntary labor supply will be inadequate to perform a necessary function. Should one move toward increasing the supply of voluntary labor for services, which seems to have been done in the United Kingdom in blood donation, or should one go into the market and begin paying for the service, in which case there may be a change in the quality of the service itself? A church faces the same problem when it goes from a lay ministry to a professional ministry, as does any charitable organization, professional society, or club, when it moves toward professionalized management. Paid labor may be more efficient in the technical sense, but something is lost in the integrative system as we move from voluntary labor, which tends to create integrative relationships, to paid labor, where the integrative relationship is almost inevitably less.

INHERITANCE

Another social phenomenon closely related to the grants economy is inheritance, which is essentially a grant from the dead to the living. Making a will has some of the aspects of setting up a foundation. A bequest, however, is a rather peculiar form of grant. It is certainly a grant to the recipient in that it increases his net worth. It can hardly be said to diminish the net worth of the donor after he is dead, except in the sense that death removes all net worth, at least in the form of worldly goods. From the recipients' point of view inheritance, even in the narrow sense of bequests, is a sizable part of the grants economy. In a society, say, in which the life expectancy is 70 and in which there is equal distribution of wealth among age groups, about one-seventieth of the total wealth of the society will be passed on by death and inheritance in each year. If the capital-income ratio is about 3, then inheritance would account for about three-seventieths, or about 4 percent of total income in each year. Since the aged are wealthier than the young, the proportion should be more than this—perhaps as much as 8 to 10 percent. We know very little about the distribution of receipts from inheritance, although this is something that would certainly be amenable to statistical investigation.

A very important question in the dynamics of society is whether inheritance concentrates wealth or diffuses it. It may very easily do either, depending on the habits of willmaking and the legal and tax structure. The decision-making processes involved in bequests have received astonishingly little attention from economists or other social scientists. There is a certain amount of practical legal knowledge involved, and there are even training schools that train fund raisers for colleges and other institutions to advise potential will makers on how to avoid taxation, in the hope perhaps that some of the taxation that is avoided will come to the advisory institution in the form of a bequest.

The theory of the bequest should not be very different in principle from the theory of grants in general, with the one proviso that the will contemplates a situation in which the grant is compulsory and its total amount is determined simply by the total net assets of the testator. The decision-making process involves only the distribution of this total among various possible recipients. This is going to depend mainly on the system of benevolence and malevolence—that is, on the nature of the integrative structure and the identification of the testator with others. The frequency with which bequests go to children and other relatives is a testimony to the powerful integrative structure of the family. On the other hand, there may also be malevolence, as when an erring child is "cut off with a shilling," or when the threat of disinheritance is used as a motivator to extract tribute from a potentially erring child. There are some very interesting behavioral problems here that have been studied very little. I have no figures on the proportion of total inheritance in each year that goes to family members, but it must be very large. Indeed, James Morgan has concluded that the family is by far the largest component of the grants economy.[11] It is a useful indicator of the integrative norms of society that all societies have laws about the disposition of estates left intestate, almost universally leaving them to blood relations. Inheritance taxation can likewise be regarded as an expression of these norms, representing the claims of the state against the family, or private charities, on the total of inheritance grants.

Inheritance has a larger aspect than that of the mere bequest of worldly goods. Each of us inherits from our parents language, culture, and class as well as the genetic attributes of race, genetic defects such as leukemia, and, more doubtfully, genetic excellences. We inherit also from the society around us cathedrals, literature, pictures, music, the great achievements of the past that are part of our heritage. The principle of serial reciprocity comes into play here, for those who are aware of this inheritance acquire a sense of community with the past and hence also with the future; they become concerned not only with conserving but also with increasing the inheritance that is passed on to the next generation. There may be very sharp personal psychological differences among individuals and among societies in the extent to which this sense of inheritance and obligation to the past is felt. If childrearing and educational processes are traumatic, the debt to the past may not be felt at all except as a burden, and there would be no interest in conserving it or passing it on.

Just as there is a problem in the impact of inheritance on the distribution of wealth, so also in the larger sense inheritance may perpetuate, increase, or diminish existing inequalities. The fact that I inherited the English language from my parents and teachers and peers is an asset to me in that English is a world language, which somebody who inherited Welsh or Basque would have to acquire by investment of both time and money. Knowledge of the English language probably has a monetary value for the individual that could conceivably be estimated. Similarly, I may inherit a religion, a nationality, and a culture, which may be of more or less value to me, and the differential inheritance of these things may easily lead toward increasing or decreasing inequality, depending on the nature of the process itself. If inheritance leads to inequality, it may be necessary to intervene where increasing equality is a social goal. We can think of Head Start and similar remedial measures as almost equivalent to negative inheritance taxation—that is, as a kind of negative tax or subsidy to those whose cultural or genetic inheritance is in some sense deficient.

It is clear that the one-way transfer, far from being something extraneous or extraordinary in the general organization of social life, is an integral and essential part of the system, without which not only community but organization and society itself would be virtually impossible. The concentration of economists on exchange as a social organizer, important as that is, has frequently blinded them to this essential fact.

NOTES

1. A decision is a complex phenomenon that involves at least two elements. First, there is a selection of one from at least two alternative images of the future present in the mind of the decision maker; second is the decision maker's selection of an act that he believes can bring about the chosen image of the future. Of course, the decision maker can be in error, in which case he will be surprised at the outcome. If he learns from his surprise, his future images and future decisions will be affected.

2. See K. E. Boulding, *Economic Analysis*, 4th ed., 2 vols. (New York: Harper & Row, 1966), 12:60-67.

3. If $x_a = 100$ bushels, at a price of $4 per bushel, it would be worth $400. If it is worth 4 utils per bushel ($v_a = 4$), its total value is 400 utils ($x_a v_a$), a "util" being a hypothetical unit of welfare. This illustration assumes simple additivity of utilities. More complex relations can be postulated but would not change the results much.

4. Kenneth E. Boulding, "Notes on a Theory of Philanthropy," in *Philanthropy and Public Policy*, ed. F. G. Dickenson (New York: National Bureau of Economics Research, 1962); reprinted in Kenneth E. Boulding, *Collected Papers*, ed. Fred Glahe (Boulder: Colorado Associated University Press, 1971), 2:235-49.

5. Alvin W. Gouldner, "The Norm of Reciprocity: A Preliminary Statement," *American Sociological Review* 25 (1960):161–78.

6. Joseph Schumpeter, *Capitalism, Socialism and Democracy* (New York: Harper & Row, 1942).

7. Arbitrage is the process by which individuals take advantage of price differences in different parts of a market by buying something where the price is low and selling it to a part of the market where the price is high. This tends to raise the price where it is low and lower it where it is high, and so bring all prices in the market into consistency. A person who practices arbitrage is called an arbitrageur.

8. Walter Y. Oi, "The Economic Cost of the Draft," *American Economic Review*, May 1967, pp. 39-62.

9. R. M. Titmuss, *The Gift Relationship* (London: Allen & Unwin, 1971).

10. The principle that "Bad money drives out the good" is usually called Gresham's law after Sir Thomas Gresham (1519?-1579).

11. James N. Morgan and Nancy A. Baerwaldt, "Trends in Inter-Family Transfers," in *Surveys of Consumers, 1971–72*, ed. Lewis Mandell (Ann Arbor: Survey Research Center, Institute for Social Research, University of Michigan, 1973) p. 20.

3

Grants and the Total Economy

THE TOTAL ECONOMY

The total economy consists of all economic conditions and transactions as they spread out over time and space. This is an immensely large and complex system. It consists of the 4.25 billion human beings of the world and all populations of economically significant artifacts, living organisms, and organizations that range over houses and household goods, food, clothing, automobiles, machines, factories, livestock, crops, garbage, waterways, money, stocks, bonds, futures contracts, taxes, corporations, labor unions, governments and government departments, regulations, and all human occupations. The list is very long. We cannot have any exact image of this fine structure of the total economy in our minds. We can, however, develop simplified models of it that help us to understand it and to understand its movement through time and the effects of specific changes in it, although our understanding can never encompass the enormous complexity of the "minute particulars" as the poet Blake called them, which constitute the real world. Grants are part of this in all their complexity and variety. For different purposes all sorts of subsets of the total economy are significant—national economies, local economies, and so on—as well as particular clusters of people involved in organizations.

THE GREAT MATRIX

The simplest model of the total economy is that of a matrix, which at least enables us to comprehend in some degree the structure of all relationships between two parties. This is illustrated in Figure 3.1. Along

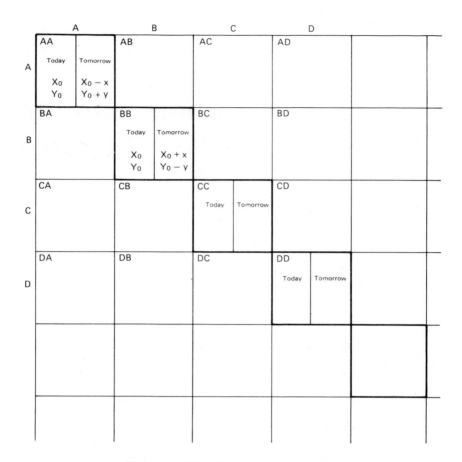

Figure 3.1 The World Economy Matrix

the top and down the sides we list all the 4.25 billion people in the world—
A, B, C, D, and so on, to the last one. If each square were an inch in size, the
total matrix would be a square of about 71,000 miles on each side in order
to get all of the people on earth in it. This is the "great matrix," almost three
times the circumference of the earth itself, so it is a very large matrix
indeed! Fortunately, the most general properties of large matrices can be
studied in small ones. Each square of the matrix we will call a cell. Diagonal
cells marked AA, BB, CC, and DD can be used to describe the economic
condition or position statement of the parties concerned. The other
squares can be used to describe the transactions or flows between the
parties. We will suppose that the flows come from the party in the row in
which the square lies to the party in the column in which it lies. Thus, in a

square labeled AB, we will put everything that flows from A to B, and in the square labeled BA everything that flows from B to A.

Suppose now that in diagonals AA, BB, and so on, we divide each square into two parts, one for today and one for tomorrow. This is the link to dynamics. Suppose now that there is an item in the square AB, x, which flows from A to B. In A's position statement of today suppose a quantity of x is $_aX_0$; then tomorrow this is $(_aX_0 - x)$. In B's position statement in square BB today's quantity is $_bX_0$; tomorrow's is $(_bX_0 + x)$. In this case x is a pure grant from A to B. If now A and B exchange x for y, then we have y in the square BA. If A starts today with an amount of $_aY_0$, tomorrow it will be $(_aY_0 + y)$. In square BB, B starts today with $_bY_0$ and tomorrow has $(_bY_0 - y)$. When there are no grants elements in the transaction, then the total value of both A's and B's position today and tomorrow is the same, for in value x equals y. When there is a grants element, x is not equal to y; if x is more than y, A's net worth will decrease and B's increase. The quantities x and y can stand for anything that is economically significant—commodities, securities, money, labor time, and so on.

Another significant factor in the matrix is production and consumption. This can be represented in the position statements down the diagonal—production by an increase in something and consumption by a diminution in something between today and tomorrow. These changes are internal and not caused directly by flows in or out. Production of one thing, furthermore, nearly always involves the consumption of others—raw materials out of which it is made; the food, clothing, housing, and machinery that the person making it consumes between today and tomorrow; and so on. There may also be production or consumption of securities and money and, of course, of persons as well as of commodities, as people die and are born.

An important key to the dynamics of the matrix is that the transactions reflect decisions, which are in some sense agreed to or at least accepted by the two parties involved. The decisions in turn are determined primarily by people's perception of their position today and their potential position tomorrow and at some other future dates, in the light of the opportunities in the perceived environment, whether the exchange environment, the financial environment, or the grants environment.

THE THREE-PARTY MATRIX

We cannot even describe, much less explore, the properties of the huge matrix of the total world economy. We can, however, explore the properties of smaller and simpler matrices, which can throw some light on the properties of the great matrix of Figure 3.1. In Figure 3.2, matrix (i), we

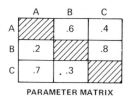

	A	B	C
A		.6	.4
B	.2		.8
C	.7	. .3	

PARAMETER MATRIX

(Proportion of total expenditures allocated to each of the recipient parties)

	A	B	C	Exp	Bal
A	100	54	36	−90	−48
B	14	100	56	−70	− 4
C	28	12	100	−40	+52
Rec	42	66	92	200	0

(i)

	A	B	C	Exp	Bal
A	52	25	17	−42	+35
B	13	96	53	−66	−13
C	64	28	152	−92	−22
Rec	77	53	70	200	0

(ii)

	A	B	C	Exp	Bal
A	87	46	31	−77	−17
B	11	83	42	−53	+14
C	49	21	130	−70	+ 3
Rec	60	67	73	200	0

(iii)

	A	B	C	Exp	Bal
A	70	36	24	−60	+ 4
B	13	97	54	−67	− 9
C	51	22	133	−73	+ 5
Rec	64	58	78	200	0

(iv)

	A	B	C	Exp	Bal
A	74	38	26	−64	+ 3
B	12	88	46	−58	+ 3
C	55	23	138	−78	− 6
Rec	67	61	72	200	0

(v)

	A	B	C	Exp	Bal
A	77	40	27	−67	− 5
B	12	91	49	−61	+ 1
C	50	22	132	−72	+ 4
Rec	62	62	76	200	0

(vi)

	A	B	C	Exp	Bal
A	72	37	25	−62	+ 3
B	12	92	50	−62	− 2
C	53	23	136	−76	− 1
Rec	65	60	75	200	0

(vii)

	A	B	C	Exp	Bal
A	75	39	26	−65	0
B	12	90	48	−60	+ 1
C	53	22	135	−75	− 1
Rec	65	61	74	200	0

(viii)

	A	B	C	Exp	Bal
A	75	39	26	−65	0
B	12	91	49	−61	0
C	53	22	134	−75	0
Rec	65	61	75	201	0

(ix)

Rule: Each party spends an amount equal to last period's receipts, in constant proportions to the other parties, as given by the Parameter Matrix.

Figure 3.2 The Three-Party Matrix with the Try-to-Balance-the-Budget Rule

suppose an economy of three parties, A, B, and C. We will suppose that the position statement in the diagonal boxes (circled) consists only of a stock of money and that the transactions consist only of transfers of money from one party to another. We can think of this either as a pure grants economy in which the transactions are simple transfers of money, or we can interpret it as transfers of money for all purposes, whether for grants or for exchange, where the things that are bought and sold for money, however, are not shown.

We start off in matrix (i) by supposing that each of the three parties has $100 in his position statement, as we see down the diagonal. In the first row of matrix (i) we see that A pays out $54 to B; $36 to C. These represent receipts to B and C; similarly for the other rows. When we sum the rows in the column marked "Exp" (expenditures), we see that A has paid out $90; B $70; and C, $40. When we sum the columns, as in the row marked "Rec" (receipts), we see that A receives $42 from the others; B, $66; and C, $92. In the column marked "Bal" (balance of payments), for each party we subtract the expenditures from the receipts, so that A pays out $48 more than he receives, B pays out $4 more than he receives, and C receives $52 more than he pays out. The sum of the receipts row or of the expenditures column is $200. These have to be equal because every dollar paid out by one person is received by another. The sum of the balances of payments similarly is zero. It represents just a shifting around of the constant cargo of money among the three parties.

In matrix (ii) we recalculate the position statements for the next period. A started off with $100 and now has $48 less, so he has $52. B started off with $100 and has $4 less, or $96. C has $52 more, or $152. Now the question arises, What behavior patterns should we assume? A great variety are possible. Let us first suppose in this case that each party tries to balance the budget by paying out (spending or giving) as much as was received in the previous period. Thus A, who received $42 in the first period, we assume will want to pay only this amount out in the second. We assume that for each party the total payment is divided between the two others in constant proportions given by the Parameter Matrix at the top of the figure. Thus, A pays out $42 × .6 = $25 to B and $42 × .4 = $17 to C. (Figures are rounded to the nearest digit.) B pays out $66 × .2 = $13 to A and $66 × .8 = $53 to C. C pays out $92 × .7 = $64 to A and $92 × .3 = $28 to B. We now recalculate the total receipts, expenditures, and balance for each and repeat the process in matrices (iii) to (ix). We see the balances diminishing, though there tends to be a swing for each party between positive and negative balances from one period to the next. By matrix (viii) we have reached a virtual equilibrium. (The rounding of the figures prevents all the balances falling to zero; a possible case is shown in matrix (ix), which will continue until the parameters change.) We notice that the money stocks are redistributed from A to B toward C.

Over a very wide range of behavioral assumptions, a system of this kind moves toward an equilibrium with what might be called the change factor, in this case, the balance of payments, declining to the point where it no longer produces behavioral change. The same process with a different behavioral assumption—that the expenditures of each party to the others is in constant proportion to the first party's money stock—is shown in Figure 3.3, with the money stocks in the diagonals as in Figure 3.2. The Parameter Matrix shows the proportions of expenditures in each cell to the corresponding money stock that will produce the initial matrix (i), with the assumption that each of the three parties starts off with $100 in money stock. This is the same as matrix (i) of Figure 3.2. A starts off with $100, with a balance of −$48, so in the period of matrix (ii) his money stock is $52. B's balance in matrix (i) is −$4, so his money stock becomes $96; C's balance is $52, so his money stock becomes $152. Expenditures then are calculated in matrix (ii) according to the proportions of the Parameter

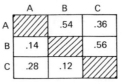

	A	B	C
A	////	.54	.36
B	.14	////	.56
C	.28	.12	////

PARAMETER MATRIX

	A	B	C	Exp	Bal
A	100	54	36	−90	−48
B	14	100	56	−70	− 4
C	28	12	100	−40	+52
Rec	42	66	92	200	0

(i)

	A	B	C	Exp	Bal
A	52	28	19	−47	+ 9
B	13	96	54	−67	−21
C	43	18	152	−61	+12
Rec	56	46	73	175	0

(ii)

	A	B	C	Exp	Bal
A	61	33	22	−55	+ 2
B	11	75	42	−53	0
C	46	20	164	−66	− 2
Rec	57	53	64	173	0

(iii)

	A	B	C	Exp	Bal
A	63	34	23	−57	0
B	11	75	42	−53	0
C	46	19	162	−65	0
Rec	57	53	65	174	0

(iv)

Rule: Each party expends to the others an amount equal to the first party's money stock, multiplied by the corresponding proportions in the Parameter Matrix.

Figure 3.3 The Three-Party Matrix with Spend-a-Constant-Proportion-of-the-Money-Stock Rule

Matrix. These processes are repeated to get matrices (iii) and (iv). We see that we approach an equilibrium of the balances very rapidly, which is approximately matrix (iv). It is interesting to note that in this case, while the money stock remains constant, the total of expenditures and receipts falls because the money stock is redistributed toward the low spender, C.

In Figure 3.4 we see a case that does not produce an equilibrium but a constant fluctuation. We start in matrix (i), the same as matrix (i) of Figure 3.2. Here, however, we suppose a behavior in which each party tries to balance its particular budget with each other party. That is, each party in the next period pays out to the other parties what thay paid in to it in the first period. Thus, in the first period A pays out $54 to B but only receives $14 from B. In the second period, matrix (ii), then, A pays out $14 to B, but B pays out $54 to A. The matrix has simply reversed itself across the diagonal. In the next period matrix (iii) simply reverts to matrix (i) again, and this will go on indefinitely. This, of course, is a very unlikely case, but it

	A	B	C	Exp	Bal
A	100	54	36	−90	−48
B	14	100	56	−70	− 4
C	28	12	100	−40	+52
Rec	42	66	92	200	0

(i)

	A	B	C	Exp	Bal
A	52	14	28	−42	+48
B	54	96	12	−66	+ 4
C	36	56	152	−92	−52
Rec	90	70	40	200	0

(ii)

	A	B	C	Exp	Bal
A	100	54	36	−90	−48
B	14	100	56	−70	− 4
C	28	12	100	−40	+52
Rec	42	66	92	200	0

(iii)

Rule: Try to balance the budget with *each* party.
Total expenditure = Last period's receipts (Each expends to party X what he got from X the last time)

Figure 3.4 The Particular Balances Rule

illustrates the folly of trying to achieve particular balances between pairs of individuals or even nations.

STABILITY AND EQUILIBRIUM IN THREE-PARTY MATRICES

The stability of the system depends a great deal on the parameters in the Parameter Matrix. Thus, in Figure 3.2 when total receipts or expenditures are constant at $200, this is because the paremeters in each row of the Parameter Matrix add up to 1.0, so that each party spends the whole of last year's income. It can be shown that if the parties together spend more than their last year's income, that income would continually rise in dollar terms. If the corresponding commodity transfers do not change, this means that commodity prices as a whole will rise and there will be inflation. Similarly, if the total expenditures are less than the income of last year, there will be a constant deflation of money incomes and, if the commodity transactions do not change, a deflation of prices. These cases can be worked out in the exercises at the end of this chapter.

Many behavior rules can be postulated that would lead the system away from equilibrium, such as "increase your expenditures after a negative balance, and decrease expenditures after a positive balance," but these would be even more extreme than the case of Figure 3.4 and are unlikely in simple balance-of-payments matrices. When it comes to the great matrix of Figure 3.1, which includes production and consumption, of course, "development" is a movement away from equilibrium in the net worth as a result of accumulation—that is, as production exceeds consumption both in goods and in human knowledge, which increases productivity. Even here, however, balances of payments as a whole rarely fail to move toward an equilibrium, though there may be individual bankruptcies and defaults of debt.

THE PURE GRANTS MATRIX AND THE ECHO EFFECT

The very simple models postulated above suggest that even a pure grants economy would reach an equilibrium under quite reasonable assumptions in which there is not much overall change in the distribution of cash balances. This does not preclude changes in the equilibrium position itself because of the change in the parameters of the system. In Figures 3.2 and 3.3, for instance, the equilibrium position is a result of the parameters specified in the Parameter Matrix. If these were different, the equilibrium position would be different. Nevertheless, a fundamental principle is involved here that neither negative nor positive balances of payments can go on for very long. Otherwise, those parties having a negative balance of payments will run out of money completely and will not be able to make any further payments. Those who have positive balances will find that they have too much money and will want to unload it.

Even three-party models illustrate a very important proposition—that when things work themselves out in the fine structure, there is a sequence of the effects of the behavior of one party on other parties, the other parties' reactions to this behavior, and so on. This often continues through to some kind of equilibrium, the end results of which may be very different from the initial conditions.

We see this even in the grants economy. Suppose, for instance, that the matrix of Figure 3.2 represents pure grants without anything passing in return. Thus, in Figure 3.2, matrix (i), we see that A pays B $54 and receives from B $14, so that A's net grant to B is $40. Similarly, A's net grant to C is ($36 − $28), or $8; B's net grant to C is ($56 − $12), or $44. The overall net grant is the same as the balances in Figure 3.2, matrix (i), that is, it represents the immediate loss or gain in net worth. A loses $48, B loses $4, and C gains $52. When we reach equilibrium, however, in Figure 3.2, matrix (ix), we see that for each party the net grant to the others is zero: A gives $39 − $12 = $27 to B, and gets $53 − $26 = $27 from C, and similarly for the others. However, comparing (ix) with (i), we see that there has been a change in the net worth (in this case, money stock): −$25 for A, −$9 for B, and +$34 for C. This represents what might be called an equilibrium grants structure over the processes that have gone on since matrix (i); A and B end up making grants to C, fundamentally because A and B are bigger spenders than C. A species of implicit grant is involved in the redistribution of money stocks as a result of shifts from one equilibrium to another. Thus, in an equilibrium A has lost less ($25 rather than $48), B has lost more ($9 rather than $4), and C has gained a little less ($34 rather than $52) than in the first transaction of matrix (i) because of the interconnectedness of the whole system. This might be called the echo effect, as the impact of a particular transaction echoes and reechoes in other transactions through the system.

EXPECTATIONAL BEHAVIOR PRODUCES FLUCTUATIONS

The question as to what actual assumptions about behavior functions are most realistic, even in the case of a relatively simple balance-of-payments model like the above, is extremely difficult. Many other behavior patterns besides the two modeled above—that is, expenditures based on last period's income or receipt or expenditures based on current money stocks—could be added. Decisions, for instance, are always based on expectations about the future, and many economists have cited waves or fashions of optimism and pessimism as affecting economic behavior. Thus when people think prices are going up, they buy; when they think prices are going down, they sell. This in itself is sufficient to account for many of the irregular fluctuations in organized competitive markets, such as the wheat market or the stock market. When prices are perceived as low, people buy. This raises the price; this encourages them in the belief that prices will rise, so prices rise still further. As prices go on rising, however, they eventually become high, in people's perception, and then a fall is expected. People on balance decide to sell; this pushes down the price and so confirms the expectations—people decide to sell still more, and the price falls until it becomes low again, at which point the fluctuation begins anew.

If people expect a rise in incomes, they will spend more out of their existing income, perhaps, and draw down their money stock. Beyond a certain point, however, declining money stocks have an increasing effect; as a person's money stock approaches zero, expenditure is almost sure to be curtailed. As our models suggest, the tendency toward an equilibrum is maintained under a great variety of behavioral assumptions, although one type of behavior might dominate in one period and another in another. The supply of grants may be subject to something like the above considerations, depending on the grantor's views of the future and of the present position. The widespread expectation of the end of the world in the year 1000 seems to have produced large grants to the church toward the end of the tenth century. The Soviet Sputnik undoubtedly produced large grants to science in the United States. A new religion like Mormonism undoubtedly increased tithing and grants to churches. Nevertheless, there is also a certain stability about the grants economy, as there is about the exchange economy. It is certainly not absurd to postulate an equilibrium structure of grants with certain given parameters, even though these parameters will change over time.

THE RELATIVE PRICE STRUCTURE

A very important aspect of the great matrix is the set of relative prices. This is the matrix, over all commodities, of how much of commodity y we can get for one unit of commodity x in exchange. This matrix can be reduced to a list of prices in terms of a single exchangeable, money, from which all relative prices can easily be derived. If wheat is $4 a bushel and an automobile is $8,000, one automobile exchanges for 2,000 bushels of wheat. From Adam Smith on, economics has postulated an equilibrium set of relative prices, divergence from which produces behavior reactions that move the actual price set toward the equilibrium set. The equilibrium set is closely connected to the set of alternative costs, that is, the amount of commodity y one can produce with the resources released by sacrificing the production of one unit of commodity x. If the set of relative prices in the market, that is, in actual exchange, differs perceptibly from the set of relative alternative costs, there will be a tendency to move resources out of the production of those things that are undervalued in the market and into the production of those things that are overvalued, which will diminish the amount of the undervalued goods coming on the market, and so raise their price, and increase the quantity and lower the price of the overvalued goods.

In Adam Smith's famous example of "a nation of hunters,"[1] resources released by not catching an additional beaver could be used to catch two deer in the woods. This is the alternative cost. If in the marketplace, however, one can then get three deer for a beaver, beavers are overvalued and deer undervalued by comparison with their alternative costs in the woods. There will then be a tendency to shift resources out of deer and into beavers. So, for every two deer not caught by the shift of resources, one beaver can be caught, which can be taken to the market in exchange for three deer. Under these circumstances beaver production will expand, deer production will decline, more beaver will come to market and fewer deer, and it will not be long before in the market one beaver will be exchanged for two deer rather than three.

HOW GRANTS AFFECT RELATIVE PRICES

The grants economy can affect the relative price structure in the market by taxes and subsidies (negative taxes) levied on particular commodities, which from the point of the individual decision maker changes the structure of alternative costs. If beavers are taxed appropriately and deer are not, if a beaver exchanges for three deer in the market, even if it exchanges for two deer in the woods there would not be an expansion of the beaver industry because of the tax. By and large, commodity taxes and subsidies tend to diminish the production of taxed commodities and increase the production of the subsidized commodities. By how much, of course, depends on the elasticities, that is, the responsiveness of behaviors to the change. Thus, it is a familiar principle in economic theory that a tax on a commodity will not have much impact on its output if this supply and demand are inelastic, that is, if people consume or produce pretty much the same amount even though the price rises. The theory of the incidence of a commodity tax is familiar in almost every

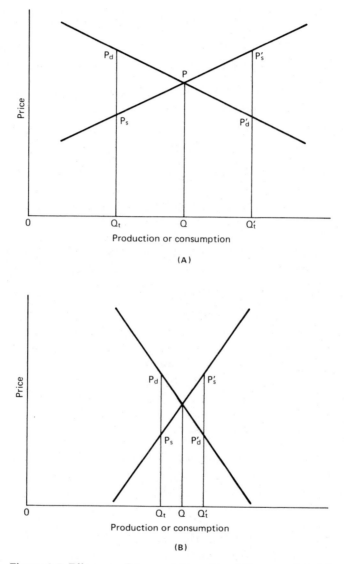

Price

P_d

P_s'

P

P_s

P_d'

0   Q_t Q Q_t'

Production or consumption

(A)

Price

P_d P_s'

P_s P_d'

0   Q_t Q Q_t'

Production or consumption

(B)

Figure 3.5 Effects on Price and Quantity of Taxes or Subsidies

economics textbook. It is essentially an application of the principles of grants economics in its impact on the relative price and output structure, as demonstrated in Figure 3.5.

In Figure 3.5A $P_dP'_d$ is the demand curve and $P_sP'_s$ the supply curve. QP is the equilibrium price in the absence of taxes or subsidies; OQ, the equilibrium amount produced or consumed. If a tax equal to P_dP_s per unit is imposed, production and consumption will shrink to OQ_t, at which the price the consumer pays is Q_tP_d, and the price the producer receives is Q_tP_s, the difference being the unit tax. Similarly, a subsidy of $P'_sP'_d$ will expand production and consumption to OQ'_t. B is the same as A except that the supply and demand curves are steeper, that is, more inelastic, the quantity produced or consumed being less affected by a change in price. The change in production or consumption, QQ_t or QQ'_t, is much less in B than in A.

Monopoly creates an implicit grant from the purchasers of the monopolized product, and ultimately through echo effects from the whole society, to the monopolistic sellers. This clearly has an important effect on the relative wage-price structure. The overall effects of monopoly may be more important in local and isolated markets, which do not attract much attention but which may add up to a fairly large total impact. Monopoly tends to arise out of economies of scale, which make large organizations, up to a point, have lower costs than small ones; under these circumstances big firms, and even states and churches, tend to gobble up the little ones, though often small organizations survive in the cracks between the big ones. Certainly in the biosphere a wide variety of sizes of organisms coexist, from blue whales to mitochondria. Since 1973 the most dramatic monopoly has been the Organization of Petroleum Exporting Countries (OPEC), which has created a large grants flow to the rulers and owners of the oil-producing countries involved, shared somewhat even by non-members. This is a rather exceptional case, not only because the payoffs for monopolistic control of an exhaustible resource like oil are very large, for with rising prices oil in the ground bears a positive rate of return as its value grows, but also because the political climate brought especially the Arab producers together in a common interest of hostility to Israel. OPEC indeed is the only international cartel that has been really successful on a large scale.

DISTRIBUTION OF NET WORTH AND INCOME

Another very important aspect of the great matrix is the distribution of both net worth and income. These two distributions are related, and if we include the capital value of the person as human capital in the net worth, they are quite closely related; the larger the net worth of a person, the larger the income. Income, whether of a person, a family, or a group, is derived from their asset structure, including the human body and mind from which labor income comes. Even then, however, the two distributions will not be quite identical because of the different rates of return on assets of different kinds and the different proportions of assets or different rates of return that individuals hold. In a sense the problem of the aggregate net worth or income of all individuals together is the same as the problem of its distribution. If we know each individual net worth or income, then we know both the aggregate and we know how it is distributed. A critical question, therefore, for both aggregates and their distribution is, What determines the growth or decline in either the net worth or the income of each individual in the matrix? The net worth of an individual increases when the value of assets increases more than the value of liabilities. When liabilities are incurred, as when the individual borrows $1,000, $1,000 is added to the liabilities in the shape of a debt obligation and added to assets in the shape of cash. The liability will grow by the rate of interest on the debt. It will decline as interest is paid or as the loan is paid off by transfers of cash to the creditor.

What happens on the asset side depends on the use that is made of the cash received. If this is used to purchase assets that grow in value, whether this is education, which increases the capital value of the person, or whether it consists of commodities, which increase in price or can be increased in quantity either by production—as, for instance, a potter may make pots—or by exchange—like a wheat speculator—then if the assets grow at a faster rate than the liabilities, the net worth will increase. The increase of assets depends on producing more than is consumed, that is, on accumulation in value terms. We are assuming here that there is some measure of value, such as indexed money, of constant purchasing power that does not itself change through inflation or deflation.

THE ROLE OF GRANTS IN DISTRIBUTION

The role of the grants economy in the distribution process is significant. As we have seen a grant is essentially a redistribution of net worth, whether direct or indirect. Even a direct grant, as we have seen, is likely to have considerable indirect effects, so that we cannot simply assume that a direct grant or transfer is the end of the matter. It will set in motion all kinds of behavior—echoes—that will involve a further redistribution of net worth. Grants may have a significant effect in the increase in net worth, both of individuals and of the aggregate. Grants to education, for instance, where these are successful, may increase the net worth of the recipients in terms of the value of the person by far more than the grant. Grants for research, for example, may increase the net worth all over society through increased knowledge or productivity. On the other hand, there may be grants that diminish net worth, such as the grants that society makes to keep unrehabilitated prisoners in jail, where they simply deteriorate, or the grants made for the purposes of war, which destroys net worth. The matrix is a vast system of echoes; a single grant echoes and reechoes through the system as it changes people's behavior, and it is often very hard to predict what the total effect will be.

INHERITANCE AS A GRANT

Another very important aspect of the great matrix is births, deaths, and aging. Something like 200,000 people die in the world every day, and about 300,000 babies are born. Every day everybody in the world is a day older. The assets of the dead have to be distributed among the living. This is inheritance and is in a sense a part of the grants economy. Most inheritance goes on in the family, although people may leave their net worth to foundations, charities, and even to governments. The pattern of inheritance has a good deal to do with the dynamics of the distribution of net worth and income. Thus, primogeniture, that is, the inheritance of the estate by the eldest son, with little going to the other children, tends to concentrate wealth, whereas equal distribution of estates, which is the principle of the *égalité* of the French Revolution, tends toward more equal distribution of wealth. There are complicating factors, however, as always. Equal distribution of estates may lead to fractionation of farms in agriculture, to small and widely dispersed parcels of land, whereas primogeniture preserves the more efficient scale of operation. Equal distribution of estates, therefore, may involve a more equal distribution of a declining total. One possible answer to this is an efficient financial system that will permit the administration of units of land or of capital of optimum size while still allowing the net worth to be more widely distributed. Thus, a farm could be inherited equally among a number of children, yet one of them who is a good farmer may administer it and the others take out their inheritance in terms of debt or perhaps even stock if the farm can be incorporated. It is one of the virtues of the corporation, indeed, that it permits equal distribution of estates without the breakup of units of administration.

The inheritance accruing to newborn babies is an interesting problem in the sense that a new baby shares the net worth of a family in some degree. It has a claim to nurturance, upbringing, and even education. This claim may in part be extended beyond the family to the community or the state. It is something that does not usually get into accounting information, but it nevertheless is highly significant. Almost any baby born in the United States has a higher net worth at the moment of birth than most babies born in Bangladesh, simply because of the larger resources of the society on which it has some kind of claim. This, in a sense, is a grant to the child from the community at large to which the newborn baby belongs, some of which is from the family, some from the larger community. This grant, of course, may be returned when the child reaches maturity or may be passed on by inheritance to future children. On the other hand, if we have a community in which population is increasing with a fixed resource or capital base, then the grant to the newborn child diminishes the net worth of the rest of the community, which gets poorer, unless this is offset by increased productive accumulation.

UNEMPLOYMENT AND INFLATION

Perhaps the most difficult problem in all of economics is the relation between unemployment and inflation or deflation. Inflation is a situation in which the general level of money prices and wages is rising; deflation, in which this level is falling. If the total quantity of money expenditures and, therefore, as we have seen, of receipts is rising relative to what is bought with the money—that is, the purchases of goods and services—there will be inflation. The price level is roughly equal to the amount of money spent divided by the amount of goods bought. There is a real difficulty in measurement here because the goods bought are an extremely hetero-geneous collection of items, changing constantly in form and quality. Rough statistical measures can be obtained by various methods, the accuracy of which diminishes the longer the period we take. It is very hard to say what the price of a color television set was in 1920 when there was not even any equivalent of it! An increase in the quantity of money payments made or received can come either from an increase in the quantity of money itself or from an increase in the velocity of its circulation, which in turn is roughly determined by the proportion of money stock that people spend in any given period. The total amount spent equals the money stock multiplied by the velocity of circulation.

Suppose in Figure 3.3, after matrix (v), the parameters in the Para-meter Matrix suddenly doubled. All the expenditures and receipts would immediately double, and total expenditures and receipts would double; the balance of payments would be unchanged, unless the parameters changed in different proportions. Similarly, if we suppose that party A is the government and continually increases its money stock by creating money, it will increase its expenditures, which will increase the receipts of the other parties, which will increase their expenditures in turn; the increase in government money stock will gradually be redistributed to the other parties, and there will be a continual increase in the total volume of money payments. If this is not offset by a proportional increase in the quantities and commodities bought, there will be an inflation in prices and money wages. Similarly, a decline in the money stock or in the velocity of circulation will produce a decrease in money payments; and if the quantity of commodities bought does not decline, there will be a deflation in prices and wages.

If, now, there is an increase in the total volume of money payments and prices and money wages do not increase proportionately, households will be buying more goods and services from businesses, and the stocks of goods in the hands of businesses will decline. If there is any unemployment, businesses will then tend to hire more people in order to replenish these stocks, and unemployment will decline. If, however, there is no significant reserve of labor in those occupations that are expanding, employers will bid up wages and will tend to raise prices until the money payments bear roughly the same proportion to the things that are bought with money. The situation is complicated by the fact that labor is not a homogeneous mass of productive potentialities. It is a very heterogeneous collection of different occupations and skills. An expanding economy may run out of unemployed oil drillers long before it runs out of unemployed textile workers, and it is not easy to turn textile workers into oil drillers. Unemployment that results from the disparity between the structure of demands for different kinds of labor and the proportion of the labor force in these different skills and occupations is called structural unemployment. This is often quite hard to measure, and unless constantly recreated it will diminish as time goes on and as people adjust and learn new skills.

KEYNESIAN UNEMPLOYMENT: THE DEMAND FOR LABOR

Beyond structural unemployment there frequently exists something that has been called Keynesian unemployment because of the light that Lord Keynes threw on this particular problem.[2] Such unemployment is a result of a complex interaction among profit, interest, and money wages, as well as decisions about investment and consumption. To understand this, we have to look at what happens when somebody is employed. This is, of course, an exchange, but it looks very different from the point of view of the employer and the employee. The employer pays out money, neglecting the very rare case of barter wages, and in return he receives the time of the worker, which he can organize to produce a product. In terms of the employer's balance sheets, hiring a worker for a week reduces his liquid assets by the week's wages and increases his other assets by the product of the work, whatever that is. Unless the value of the product of the work is at least equal to the wage, the employer will be the loser by the transaction. The worker, on the other hand, gives up alternative uses of his time and receives the purchasing power of the money wage. Unless these alternative uses of time are very productive, which is not usually the case, hiring the worker for the week increases the total net worth of the society, and this increase is divided between the employer and the worker. A further complication is that where there is a market for loans, what the employer gives up is not just the money that is paid out in the wage but the interest that might have been earned on that money if it were put out as a loan. Unless, therefore, the profit on the giving of employment—that is, the net value of the product of the work to the employer—exceeds the interest that might have been obtained by putting out the wage as a loan, by an amount sufficient to compensate the employer for the risks involved, the worker will not be hired.

The demand for labor on the part of a particular employer, therefore, may be subject to quite sharp but rather short-term fluctuations, depending on the employer's own view of the future, whether, for instance, he sees the product of the work as highly valuable and whether he sees the alternative use of the wage as profitable. The employer's image of the value of the product of the work depends to a considerable extent on the way he visualizes his own asset structure, for giving employment changes this asset structure at least at the moment toward goods and away from money or loans. If the inventories in the employer's asset structure are low, he is much more likely to hire somebody to build them up than if he perceives them as high. If he perceives that there is an unsatisfied demand for capital goods—houses, machines, factories, and so on—there will be a strong demand to hire people to build these things. If on the other hand, the perception is that profits are low and that the stocks of goods are excessive and interest rates are high, the demand for labor will correspondingly shrink.

Keynesian Unemployment: The Role of Wage-Rates

The answer of neoclassicial economics to the problem of unemployment is that it is a sign that money wages are too high and if only wages would fall, employment would rise. This is shown in Figure 3.6, where we plot the amount of employment on the horizontal axis and the money wage on the vertical axis. It supposes that there is a demand for labor, DD_1; if the relevant labor force is OE, at the wage equal to EW everybody will be employed. Suppose now that there is a decline in the demand for labor to $D'D'_1$; then at the old wage the amount of employment would be only E_1 and the unemployment equal to E_1E. In classical theory unemployment would lower the wage at which people were willing to work, say, EW_2, and unemployment would be eliminated. This solution, however, as Lord Keynes pointed out, has serious flaws. In the first place there are institutional obstacles to the lowering of money wages, especially where there are trade union contracts. Second, even if there is a lowering of money wages, the echo effects that we have seen around the matrix of the system

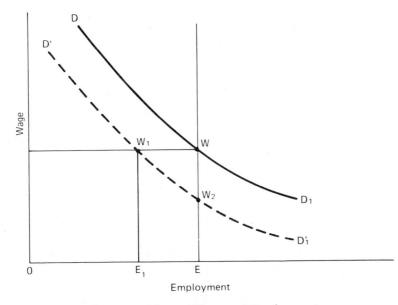

Figure 3.6 Money Wages and Employment

may reduce prices, and hence real wages may not be lowered and profits may not be raised, and so unemployment would continue. The only answer under those circumstances would be an increase in the total volume of expenditure and receipts, either through an increase in the money stock or an increase in the velocity of circulation, which would expand the demand for labor again and, if the money wage did not increase, would increase employment.

THE UNEMPLOYMENT-INFLATION DILEMMA

Increasingly we are running into another dilemma—that the attempt to solve the unemployment problem by essentially monetary means results in inflation, and not only inflation but accelerating inflation, which is very dangerous. We saw this particularly in the 1970s, when the slowdown in the rate of increase in productivity to the point where at the end of the 1970s productivity was actually declining coupled with the formation of OPEC and the exaction of monopoly prices for oil, plus an increased willingness on the part of governments to run budget deficits, had produced almost the world over what looks like an accelerating inflation. In the United States, by 1980, it had reached more than 10 percent per annum, which would mean a doubling of the price level every seven years, even if the rate of inflation did not increase. In Israel it reached 130 percent per annum. Even socialist Yugoslavia had about the highest inflation rate in Europe.

Lord Keynes himself was aware of the problem, which he described as the "bottlenecks" problem, arguing that as the demand for labor of different kinds rose under the impulse of expanded money demands, and increased money expenditures and receipts, then in one industry after another full employment of a particular kind of labor would be reached after which point wages would rise sharply. This is shown in Figure 3.7, with the same axes as Figure 3.6. We start out with a demand for labor $D_1D'_1$, wage E_1W_1, and unemployment, let us say, in this particular area equal to E_1E_3. Then we suppose an increase in the money demand for labor to $D_2D'_2$ as a result of an expansion of the monetary system. The supply of labor is extremely elastic when there is unemployment, so the wage will not rise much, only to E_2W_2. At this point, however, something close to full employment is reached in this particular occupation, and if the demand for labor increases beyond this, say, to $D_3D'_3$, the wage will rise very sharply to E_3W_3. Employment will only rise a little; there may indeed be a labor shortage and it will be hard to get people. Then if the demand for labor rises beyond this to D_4, the wage will rise without any increase in employment, and, of course, there will be a corresponding rise in the

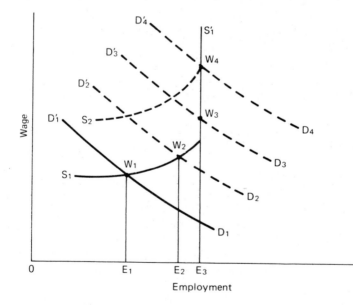

Figure 3.7 The Bottlenecks Problem

prices of goods, so real wages may not rise at all. Even if the supply curve of labor shifts backward, as it is likely to do under the impact of inflation from $S_1S'_1$ to $S_2S'_1$, we see this may not really change the situation very much at the point W_4, the point at which the increase in the money payments in dollar terms produces inflation rather than an expansion of employment. This can happen overall long before we reach an optimum level of employment, while there is still unemployment in many occupations.

The problem is enormously complicated by the large number of echo effects around the great matrix. Thus, there may be a spontaneous increase in either wages or prices as a result of a sudden access of monopoly power. The increase in the price of oil due to OPEC is a good example of this. This in turn may increase other wages, other prices. It may increase money payments and may itself increase the money supply through, for instance, the stimulation of budget deficits or expansionary banking policy, which justifies the original increase in prices or wages. This may encourage further increase in prices or wages, which is again justified by an increase in the money supply, and so we go on. Any attempt to stop the inflation under these circumstances, however, can easily produce unemployment because of the inflexibility of the money price and wage downward. Inflation, indeed, is a little bit like heroin—it can easily become addictive.

THE ROLE OF FINANCIAL MARKETS: INTEREST VERSUS PROFIT

Another contribution to the complexity of the situation is what happens in financial markets and interest rates. The real rate of interest is roughly equal to the nominal rate minus the rate of inflation. If I borrow $100 at 15 percent, I pay back $115 next year. If in the interval there has been a 12 percent inflation, that $115 is roughly worth only $103 of what I sacrificed, so that the real rate of interest is approximately 3 percent. More exactly, it would be $3 \times 100/112$, or about 2.7 percent. It is important to recognize that a very important condition behind the employer's state of mind when he hires somebody is the real rate of interest that he might get on the money paid out in the wage compared with the real rate of profit that he gets by employing the worker. In the early stages of inflation, financial markets frequently do not react to it, so that nominal rates of interest are sticky and the real rate of interest falls. This was particularly noticeable in the United States between about 1950 and 1965. In the late 1960s, however, nominal rates started to rise very sharply to offset the inflation, so that real rates of interest started to rise, although in many assets like savings accounts that did not adjust the real rate of interest was negative, as the rate of inflation was higher than the nominal rate.

Inflation and deflation also have an important effect on profits. Profits are made by buying something at one time, transforming it in some way, and selling it at a later time for more than was paid out in acquiring and producing it. In an inflation most prices are rising all the time, so that the price at which the profit maker sells has a much better chance of being higher than the price or the costs at which it was bought. In a deflation the reverse is the case. Inflation, therefore, tends to create profits and shifts distribution toward them; deflation shifts distribution away from profits and, if interest rates are not flexible downward, as they often are not, toward interest.

We saw this spectacularly in the Great Depression of the 1930s. There was a great deflation from 1929 to 1933 in which in the United States the money value of the national income was almost halved. In 1932 and 1933 profits were negative, perhaps 2 or 3 percent, and real interest was still positive at perhaps 3 percent, so that in those years it is almost literally true that anyone who gave employment lost money by it, and he could have done better by putting the money not paid in wages out to interest. It is not surprising, therefore, that unemployment in 1932/33 was 25 percent of the labor force; it was remarkable that it was not even higher. Indeed, the only thing that kept the economy going at all was sheer habit, the desire to hold enterprise together, and the hope of better things to come.

INFLATION AND THE RACE BETWEEN INTEREST AND PROFIT

Now we find ourselves in a somewhat contrary situation with rising rates of inflation. There is a kind of race between real interest and real profit. Inflation reduces the real rate of interest from any given nominal rate, but the nominal rate continues to rise to try to catch up. Inflation also shifts national income into profits and increases the nominal profit rate, but it also diminishes the real profit rate by comparison with the nominal rate, just as it does with interest. The favorable effect of inflation on employment, therefore, may depend on the fact that it is not well anticipated, especially in financial markets, so that interest rates do not catch up and a gap appears between profits and interest that is favorable to an increase in employment.

If, however, financial markets do catch up—and there are alarming signs that they are doing so—a given rate of inflation may have a diminishing effect on the demand for labor, and an accelerating inflation is necessary to sustain full employment. This is a catastrophic situation that can only lead to hyperinflation, as indeed happened in Germany in 1923 and Hungary in 1946 when the price level doubled every few days and people simply ran from the pay window to the store to spend their money as fast as they possibly could before it lost its value. This is hardly conducive to good economic decisions.

INFLATION, DEFLATION, AND THE RELATIVE WAGE-PRICE STRUCTURE

Even this somewhat extended discussion of the inflation-unemployment problem by no means covers all the complexities. Another aspect, for instance, is the disproportions that develop in deflation and, perhaps to a lesser extent in inflation, in the set of relative prices and in the distribution of incomes. In the Great Depression of the 1930s, for example, agricultural prices fell roughly in proportion to the decline in money incomes and money payments, so that agriculture production and employment in agriculture did not decline—in fact, even rose a little. The money income of farmers, however, was about halved; they produced about the same amount at roughly half the 1929 price. Their burden of debt was almost doubled, though there was remarkably little default. In the industrial sector, on the other hand, money incomes also about halved, but because prices and wages only fell by about 25 percent, output and employment also fell by about 25 percent, presumably because of certain monopolistic elements in the pricing of industrial commodities and industrial wages that did not obtain in agriculture. It can be argued indeed that if industrial money wages and prices had fallen as much as agricultural wages and prices, there would have been very little unemployment, although because of the extremely complex echo effects there is considerable doubt about this.

EFFECTS OF GRANTS ON UNEMPLOYMENT AND INFLATION

It is time now to turn to the question of the role of the grants economy in these processes of unemployment and inflation. This is highly significant but also as complex as the general problem itself. In the first place the private grants economy, which is predominantly in the family, has a profound effect in moderating the impact of unemployment on consumption. Without this the unemployed would simply starve to death after they had drawn whatever savings they might have, which is usually not very much, as unemployment tends to affect the more marginal workers who are also the most poverty-stricken ones. So there develops a large intrafamily grants economy—wives go out to work when husbands lose their jobs, people move in with relations when they can no longer afford to pay rent, and so on. The public grants economy also plays an important role here insofar as it develops poor relief, unemployment insurance, and so on.

If unemployment insurance is very generous, as the Canadians found some years ago, it may well increase nominal unemployment simply because people take advantage of the opportunity for a little vacation—by living on their unemployment insurance. If the demand for leisure is high, this may even add to the general welfare. Involuntary unemployment, however, is always a loss to society, and it is a high social priority to eliminate it. Whether the public grants economy, through taxes and subsidies (including welfare payments), can eliminate it and at the same time avoid inflation, is one of the great question marks of our age. Up to now, we certainly have not succeeded in resolving the inflation-unemployment dilemma. We may have to look to a combination of well-devised public grants in terms of taxes and subsidies together with some form of workable regulation that would prevent spontaneous increases in money wages, money prices, or interest rates. Such increases often force a further inflation to offset them without creating unemployment.

A critical, though quite difficult, question is the role of monopoly in these spontaneous price, wage, and interest rate increases. Certainly a new monopoly will have the effect of raising money prices of the monopolized commodity, and a newly successful labor union is likely to raise money wages. Whether old monopolies, whether in commodity or labor markets, are likely to be leaders in raising money prices or wages is a more difficult question. There is some evidence, for instance, that in moderate inflations, like that of World War II, wages in the organized sector of the market rose more slowly than those in unorganized markets under overfull employment, simply because collective bargaining takes much more time than individual bargaining. Similarly, even in the recovery from the Great Depression in the 1930s, prices rose quite sharply in the competitive speculative markets, like wheat, even when unemployment was still over 15 percent, while prices in the more monopolistic sector rose very little. There is nothing new about the inflation-unemployment dilemma. Nevertheless, there may well be circumstances in which the more monopolistic and organized markets respond more rapidly to increases in money demand than the more competitive markets, and we may be increasingly moving into this situation.

GRANTS TO PREVENT WAGE AND PRICE INCREASES

Regulation and control, fortunately, is not the only possible answer to the prevention of undesirable money wage, price, and interest changes. Grants here may have a role in changing the motivations for raising money wages, prices, and interest rates. Proposals have been suggested—for instance, for marketable wage subsidies issued by the government.[3] These could be issued in the form of certificates, the possession of which would give the employer a subsidy in some proportion to his wage bill. Such certificates could be marketed or auctioned so that the people who would most benefit from them would bid them away from the people who would not be benefited. There have also been proposals for extra taxes on income derived from increases in money wages or money prices to be devoted to subsidizing those who decrease money wages and money prices. Something like this was proposed as early as 1960 by Gardiner Means,[4] and the idea has been elaborated by Abba Lerner and David Colander.[5] None of these schemes has actually been tried; whether they would work is still a matter of considerable dispute, but our failure to find other solutions to the problem certainly suggests that no proposal should go unexplored.

TAXES ON MONEY

There have also been proposals, usually rising from the underworld of economics and rarely accepted by its official practitioners, for taxes on the holding of money itself—taxes, for instance, on bank deposits supplemented with "depreciating stamp money" in the form of bills that have to have a stamp affixed each week so that they can retain their legal tender. Something like this was even tried in Alberta in the 1930s, apparently, with some rather unforeseen success as the stamped money became a collector's item and brought in considerable revenue to the province. Under some circumstances, this is a conceivable answer to the dilemma posed by Lord Keynes that there may be a lower limit on the nominal rate of interest imposed by the fact that money can be held at a zero interest rate, with all its psychological advantages of liquidity. If money itself had a negative nominal interest rate, without inflation, this might lower the incentive to give money a negative interest rate through inflation. A hundred dollar bill, if you hold it for a year in today's inflation, will buy considerably less at the end of the year than it would have done at the beginning. It has been argued, indeed, that a steady low rate of inflation, perhaps about 2 percent per annum, would act as a tax on idle money and would be relatively harmless. The other view is that even a little inflation always leads to more, and the only permanent solution to inflation is to have no inflation at all.

IMPLICIT GRANTS IN INFLATION AND DEFLATION

Both inflation and deflation produce a complex system of implicit grants, though the exact impact is very hard to discover. Inflation diminishes and deflation increases the real value in terms of purchasing power of actual money stocks. Inflation, therefore, redistributes net worth toward those who hold small money stocks and away from those who hold large ones, and deflation does the reverse. Inflation may redistribute toward those whose assets arise out of profits and away from those whose assets and income come from interest, although, as we have seen, this depends to some extent on the flexibility of the capital markets. In the short run, the effects may be very different from the long run.

Inflation that results from budget deficits on the part of governments is itself a form of taxation, an implicit grant from the citizens to the government. With the new money that it creates the government buys goods and services and withdraws these from the civilian population, giving instead money that depreciates in value. It is not surprising that inflation is an almost universal accompaniment of war because wars almost always produce budget deficits. Nobody wishes to pay for them honestly! A progressive tax system, as long as it is maintained, is a safeguard against inflation beyond a certain point simply because as inflation proceeds, money incomes rise and an increasing number of people get into the upper-income brackets and have to pay higher taxes. With a progressive tax system, therefore, inflation raises the average tax payment and, hence, unless there is corresponding expansion of expenditure, will reduce budget deficits.

THE GRANTS-POLITICS OF INFLATION

Very tricky questions are involved when attempts are made to protect people from inflation by so-called indexing. Without this, of course, inflation involves redistribution away from people with relatively fixed incomes, who are often pensioners and the aged. This can sometimes be a very significant implicit grant, mostly from the aged toward the middle-aged. If, however, pensions—and even more if interest payments—are indexed, that is, if the money payments rise proportionally to the price of goods and services, this may actually accelerate the rate of inflation. In the case of government pensions indexing is likely to increase public expenditures in proportion to the inflation and so increase the deficits, which are the fuel of the inflation. The redistributive effects of inflation, that is, the grants economics aspects, is often the major reason for it. We have inflation if everybody wants more than there is and thinks he can get it. One way to fudge this is to increase the number of dollars without increasing the quantity of goods. The redistribution of net worth and incomes that results is often a redistribution away from the politically weak, such as the aged and the near poor, toward the politically stronger middle-aged and middle class. Even the great Hungarian hyperinflation after World War II has been defended on the grounds that it redistributed income toward public investment in a way that could never have been done through the tax system.

I must apologize for the difficulty of this chapter. It reflects the extraordinary complexity of the problem, to which there are no easy answers. An understanding of the role that grants play in the great matrix and the whole overall economic process is, however, critical, not only to the understanding of the process itself but for the finding of any solution to the remarkably difficult problems involved.

EXERCISES

1. Begin with matrix (i) in Figure 3.2 and construct nine subsequent matrices following the rule that each party spends 10 percent more than it did in the previous period, following the proportions of the Parameter Matrix of Figure 3.2.
2. Repeat exercise 1, with each party spending 10 percent less than it did in the previous period.
3. What behavior patterns might be invoked that would bring the inflation in exercise 1 or the deflation in exercise 2 to an end?
4. Begin with matrix (i) and the Parameter Matrix of Figure 3.3 and develop nine subsequent matrices on the assumption that in each period each parameter of the Parameter Matrix is multiplied by the ratio

$$\frac{\text{total expenditures of the period}}{\text{total expenditures of the previous period}}$$

Would the pattern of the result have been different if the initial parameter matrix had been different. If so, how?
5. Begin with matrix (i) and the Parameter Matrix in Figure 3.2 but assume that each party spends a total amount in the next period equal to twice the numerical value of its balance (neglecting the minus sign). Continue for nine periods.

NOTES

1. Adam Smith, *The Wealth of Nations* (New York: Random House, Modern Library Editions), Book 1, chapter 6, p. 47.

2. J. M. Keynes, *A General Theory of Employment, Interest and Money* (New York: Harcourt Brace, 1936).

3. Richard Hazelett, *American Economic Review* 47 (1957):136–52.

4. Gardiner Means, *Pricing Power and the Public Interest: A Study Based on Steel* (New York: Harper and Brothers, 1962).

5. Abba P. Lerner and David C. Colander, *MAP: A Market Anti-Inflation Plan* (New York: Harcourt Brace Jovanovich, 1980).

4

The Implicit
Grants Economy

THE DEFINITION OF IMPLICIT GRANTS

One of the most difficult and interesting questions in the theory of the grants economy is the treatment of implicit grants. Implicit grants may be defined as redistributions of income or wealth that take place as a result of structural changes or manipulations in the set of prices and wages, licenses, prohibitions, opportunity, or access. Any change that is not a direct and explicit grant yet leads to economic redistributions is an implicit grant. There are many examples of this phenomenon, and we cannot do more than outline a few of them .

The great problem in defining implicit grants is that the concept always implies some norm or reference point in the distribution of income or wealth, divergences from which constitute the implicit grants structure. It is not even clear whether in particular cases we are referring to wealth, income, or economic welfare. If we take welfare as the most general form, then if under the distribution that is regarded as normative individual i has an economic welfare X_i, and if after some structural change in the price structure, monopoly, licensing, quotas, or anything else that will change distributions the individual has a welfare of Y_i, the implicit grant to him is $(Y_i - X_i)$. This may, of course, be a positive grant if he has an increase in welfare or a negative grant if he has a diminution. The empirical study of the implicit grants economy is difficult at both ends, for it is often difficult to agree on a norm from which divergences should be measured, and it is also frequently very difficult to estimate the actual effects of any particular change on the distribution of economic welfare. The phenomenon of the implicit grant, however, is a real one, and we cannot avoid studying it, no matter what the difficulties, without neglecting an important aspect of the real world.

The problem becomes even more difficult when we try to take account of the dynamics of the system and of distribution over time. The grants economy has an investment quality about it in the sense that the grants of one period may have an impact on the grants of the next and the subsequent periods. It is not possible to assess either the grants structure or the distributions of welfare at a point of time or in a short period of time without taking into account the impact on the future. As a very simple example of this problem, suppose we had a society in which everybody had the same total life pattern of income, so that over the whole life experience incomes were exactly equal, but in which income rose throughout life, so that all people were poor when they were young and rich when they were old. The distribution of income as measured by any conventional means during any one year would look unequal, but in fact the society would be totally egalitarian. Any income distribution of a given year, therefore, must be corrected for the past and expected future incomes of each party—an adjustment that will almost always have the effect of diminishing the degree of inequality.

The transfer of income among age groups—for example, from the middle-aged to the young and to the old—is part of the grants economy. We must regard a certain amount of this transfer as normative, although there is likely to be a range of disagreement about where the norm should lie. Further, we can assume that if the institutions in society, legal, customary, and so on, distort this distribution outside the norm, then an implicit grants system exists. For instance, if rising military budgets result in cutting short the expenditures on education to the point that the younger generation is inadequately equipped to move into the world that its elders leave, we can regard this transfer as an implicit grant away from the currently young and toward the currently middle-aged. The conceptual problems involved here are quite difficult, although inescapable, and sometimes they may have to be solved by rather arbitrary decisions about what constitutes a norm. We are likely to find ourselves with different norms for different purposes; while this is untidy, the real world is untidy, too, and must not be tidied up in the interest of overzealous intellectual housekeeping. These principles will perhaps become clearer as we examine specific cases.

MONOPOLY AS AN IMPLICIT GRANT

The first example of implicit grants is monopoly. It has long been recognized by economists that monopoly distorts the distribution of income in favor of the monopolist and may, therefore, be regarded as an implicit grant toward the monopolist and away from his customers or his potential customers, who have to pay higher prices for the monopolized commodity. Here the norm is regarded as a competitive price structure, which is also usually identified with the structure of real alternative costs. To return to Adam Smith's famous example of the beaver and the deer, the modern version of the story would be this: If giving up the production of two deer in the forests enables the hunters, with the resources released, to capture one beaver, then there is a ratio of exchange of two deer for one beaver in the woods—this is the alternative cost ratio. If the prices in the market do not correspond to this ratio, and if everybody is free and has equal opportunity either to hunt beavers or deer (this is the purely competitive situation), resources will be diverted from whatever occupation is less profitable into whatever occupation is more profitable until the market price corresponds to the alternative cost ratio. If the beaver producers then band together into a monopoly and restrict the amount of beavers coming into the market, then one beaver may exchange for more than two deer in the market. Beaver production will be unusually profitable because the monopoly is able to prevent the unfortunate deer producers from getting into the more profitable business of beaver production. Under these circumstances there is clearly an implicit grant from the deer producers to the beaver producers.

As usual, when we look at the long-run dynamics of the situation, the case becomes less clear. It may be that the security and the little surplus that the beaver producers' monopoly has enabled them to get—at the expense of the deer producers—will be used for research and development in the techniques of beaver production with a subsequent improvement in the productivity of that industry that would not otherwise have taken place. These improvements may even spill over, according to the benevolent principle of external economies,[1] into the deer industry, meaning that in the next generation everybody's productivity will have increased and everybody will be richer. In this case the implicit grants structure looks like a grant from the deer producers of one generation to the whole society of the next generation, including the children of the unfortunate deer producers of the first generation. This looks a little more defensible than the case of mere grants from deer producers to beaver producers of a single generation. Indeed, Joseph Schumpeter defended monopoly in this way, and there is certainly some evidence that highly competitive industries, such as textiles, lag in technological development and do not put much research into increasing productivity. On the other hand, industries with a certain amount of monopoly power or political power, like agriculture, that consequently have enjoyed grants, either explicit like public subsidies or implicit through monopoly prices, not infrequently use the grants to increase future productivity. All these considerations, of course, are questions rather than answers—questions that we have to ask ourselves in the real world. We cannot make any *a priori* evaluations.

TARIFFS, TAXES, AND SUBSIDIES AS IMPLICIT GRANTS

Another case that is very familiar to exchange economists is the tariff. The effect of a tariff has been analyzed extensively by neoclassical and welfare economists. Here again, the short-run redistributions are rather clear and the long-run effects are a little uncertain. A tariff is an import tax imposed on a given commodity by a country. It usually benefits the producers and injures the consumers of that commodity inside the country and injures the producers and benefits the consumers outside the country. Therefore, it represents an implicit grant from the internal consumers and the external producers to the internal producers and the external consumers. Under conditions of universal full employment it can be shown that the total benefit of the tariff is less than the total injury, meaning that we have an implicit grant with negative efficiency—that is, what is given up by the unwilling grantors is more than what is received by the recipients. Of course, if we start from a position of unemployment, the case may be different. Conceivably the tariff can result in a general increase in world output, in which case the grant will be positively efficient; that is, what is sacrificed by the grantors will be less than what is received by the grantees.

In the long run the distribution of the implicit grants may also change. If the protected industry is one with free entry, then the above-normal profits that the tariff induces will attract new firms and the industry's returns will sink to normal. Thus, it will be no better off, and the domestic consumers will be a little worse off. The foreign producers, again if there is free exit, will ultimately be no worse off, as the resources can be transferred out of the industry, returning its profitability to normal. Foreign consumers may be a little better off, and the end result may be, ironically enough, a small implicit grant from domestic consumers to foreign consumers. We frequently run into this principle, which might almost be called that of "implicit irony" because almost all acts that are designed to benefit or injure one group of people often benefit or injure other groups. For this reason, as we shall see, economic conflict is extraordinarily difficult to organize.

ECONOMIC RENT

The tariff is a special case of the enormous implicit as well as explicit grant structure implied in the system of taxes and subsidies. The problem of the ultimate incidence of taxation—that is, what is the ultimate effect of a particular tax on the distribution of economic well-being— is one of the most difficult and tangled problems in the whole of economics and is closely bound up with the whole structure of explicit and implicit grants. Neoclassical economics made some important contributions to this subject, especially in terms of more immediate and short-run impacts. The proposition, for instance, that taxes of all kinds tend to fall on economic rent and to shift from those segments of the economy that produce commodities that are elastic in demand and in supply,[2] certainly corresponds to something in the real world. A good deal of the theory of incidence of this kind can again be summed up in the proposition that what adjusts is the adjustable and that what is not adjustable has to bear the burdens of adjustment. Any change in the tax system, therefore, will tend to redistribute economic welfare in ways that will affect, for good or for ill, those who cannot adjust more than those who can. Thus, burdens fall on and benefits accrue to the receivers of economic rent simply because economic rent arises from inelastic supplies, and inelastic supplies in turn arise from the lack of adjustability—that is, the inability to transfer resources without cost.

The classical case of Ricardian rent is that in which the commodity (land) is perfectly inelastic in supply—that is, will be supplied no matter what its price or the terms of trade of its supplier. In this case all changes in net demand will fall on the supplier, whether this results from taxation or from other causes. Thus, subsidies to agriculture tend to go ultimately to landowners, especially those who owned land at the time the subsidy was inaugurated, for the subsidy will tend to be capitalized in the value of the land, the supply of land being inelastic and unadjustable, whereas the supply of farmers and farm laborers is much more elastic. Hence, a subsidy to any industry will tend to attract capital and labor into it until the returns are again normal, including the subsidy, and all the benefits of the subsidy will tend to go to the landlords. There may be important exceptions to this depressing conclusion, but there are enough examples of it to show that it cannot be brushed aside.

It is perhaps less generally recognized in traditional economics that spontaneous shifts in consumer demand, or what is more likely, shifts in government demand, also create a problem of incidence—that is, they create a pattern of implicit grants. A shift in demand from tea to coffee will create short-run[3] implicit grants from tea producers, whose incomes are reduced, to coffee producers, whose incomes are increased. In the long run, of course, the tea producers may turn over to producing coffee, or something else, but in the short run, which may last a long time, there is a real implicit grants structure. The principles of the theory of incidence apply also to this case; costs will be borne and benefits received by the receivers of economic rent.

The implicit grants structure implied by the advertising industry and the whole selling sector of the economy is of great interest and has been very little explored. Advertising is a one-way transfer of information, part of which is designed to be persuasive—that is, to change the demand structure of the society, both of private persons and of governments. It may, therefore, create an implicit grants system, resulting in transfers toward those segments of the economy that are successful in increasing the demand for their product by this method and away from those segments that are unsuccessful. I have seen very little analysis of this problem in conventional economics. Political persuasion may be equally important. Party propaganda and lobbying of interest groups constantly operate to change the structure of political power and of government expenditure, and much of this will have a redistributive effect.

QUANTITATIVE RESTRICTIONS AS IMPLICIT GRANTS

An area that is perhaps less familiar to traditional economics, but that is still well within its usual boundaries, is the distributive effect of quantitative restrictions, whether imposed by governments or by private organizations. Such restrictions as quotas, licenses, prohibitions, rationing, and direct allocations have become increasingly important instruments of both public and private policy in this century. The implicit grants, or redistributive effects, that result are enormous and often quite unrecognized and misunderstood. Any kind of quantitative restriction implies a license to some people to perform a certain activity and correspondingly a prohibition on performing it, with appropriate sanctions, for those who do not receive a license. The administration of all quantitative restrictions tends to take this form, and the effects are often very different from what the original decision makers intended.

For example, a *quota* is defined as a legal maximum amount of some activity; if the quantity of the activity is above this defined amount, the excess is illegal and is penalized. The penalties may be civil, such as fines, or criminal, such as imprisonment, and may or may not be graduated according to the amount of the excess. Thus, a country may enforce import quotas on a particular commodity so that once the specified legal amount has been imported, any further imports are illegal. There may be production quotas, as in the case of tobacco, in which each farm is allocated a certain amount that can be sold off the farm, any excess above this being illegal. The most common form of administration of a quota is a licensing system, whereby licenses to perform specific amounts of the activity are handed out or are auctioned off up to the limit that is set by law.

Rationing is a system of consumption or household purchasing quotas, the ration coupons being a license to purchase up to a certain amount. Points rationing is a variant that edges closer to a price system. A household is given a certain number of ration tickets that can be used for a specified group of commodities, at specified "points prices." Rationing can also be imposed on firms in the purchase of equipment and raw materials, in which case it is usually called a production allocation system. A prohibition, as in the case of alcoholic beverages in the United States in the 1920s, represents in effect a zero quota.

Another form of restriction that almost always produces implicit grants is wage and price control, which is frequently resorted to by governments faced with inflation. Almost the only way in which this control can be administered is to take the set of prices and wages as they existed on a certain date and freeze them, making any higher price and wage illegal. Because any particular price and wage structure becomes obsolete almost immediately and is subject to constant strain and change, an administrative apparatus has to be set up to permit exceptions. These exceptions become increasingly complex and numerous until the system finally breaks down under its own weight, at least in market-type economies. Price control in centrally planned economies is simply part of the plan. The implicit grants system involved in such centrally planned economies is extremely interesting and very little studied, but it is too complex a problem to be dealt with in this volume.

Both quantitative restrictions and price and wage control almost inevitably produce black markets where exchanges take place either in illegal quantities or at illegal prices or wages. The more complex the system of controls, the more difficult it is to police the black markets. The system is frequently eventually undermined—or those skeptical of controls might say made workable—by the development of illegality. We saw this under prohibition, as one of the most extreme cases in quantitative controls, in the development of the bootlegger and the speakeasy. This may easily lead into a general disrespect for the law and a delegitimation of political institutions, which can have disastrous consequences for a society. Another aspect of quantity and price controls is the development of corruption, another form of the illegality fostered by these controls. Where an official has the power to impose sanctions, it is often tempting to induce him to abstain from exercising power by means of bribery. This takes the form of a grants economy, as a kind of tribute, and again may lead to a disastrous delegitimation of the legal and political system. Thus, controls in effect create turnstiles; creating a turnstile is often an invitation to corrupt its attendant, and this in turn corrupts the whole system.

One of my favorite examples of the principle of implicit irony is the quota imposed by the British government on imports of Danish bacon in 1934 because of strong political pressure to "do something for British agriculture." The British pig producers persuaded the government to impose a quota on imports of Danish bacon, which had become a popular item of consumption in British families, in the hope that the diminution in imports of Danish bacon would result in an increase in demand for British bacon and, hence, a rise in its price and increased returns to the British pig industry. However, in the eyes of the British housewife the delicate and uniform Danish rashers were no substitute for the greasy and slipshod products of the British pig industry, so the demand for Danish bacon turned out to be quite inelastic. As a result of the quota the price of Danish bacon rose sharply, and the British ended up paying the Danes more money for less bacon. Thus, the quota in effect gave the Danes a very successful monopoly power in the British market. The increased demand for British bacon was small, and the net result was an implicit grant from the British consumer to the Danish producer, which was certainly not intended by the British government.[4]

Another example of the principle of implicit irony arises from the consequences of the United States tobacco quota, imposed first in 1934.[5] Under this system any farmer in the specified areas who was producing tobacco at the time received a quota—that is, a license to sell a certain amount of tobacco based on how much he had been producing. The quota in this case went to the farm rather than the farmer and very soon became a valuable property. Of two identical farms, one with a quota and one without, the farm with the quota may now sell for as much as six times the price of one that does not have a quota. It is clear that the quota represented an implicit grant—it is not quite clear from whom, perhaps from smokers who have to pay more for tobacco—to the owners of those farms that received quotas in the initial year. It may be very hard to justify this on any principle of social justice.

Another example of implicit grants in a licensing system is the issue of licences by the U.S. federal government for radio and television stations. Here again, this represents a grant from the public to the recipients of these licenses, which may easily be valued in millions of dollars. It is no secret that the fortune of President Lyndon Johnson was based in part on such an implicit grant.

Import licenses and foreign exchange control licenses are similar examples of implicit grants from the rest of society to those who are fortunate to receive the licenses. In effect, this system is one of private taxation, enabling the possessors of licenses to tax the rest of society for their own benefit. As the recipients of licenses are frequently the richer and the more powerful members of society, this type of implicit grant almost always involves redistribution from the poor to the rich and hence offsets whatever redistributions from the rich to the poor may take place through the system of direct grants and the tax system.

The licensing of people creates an implicit grants structure, just as does the licensing of property, although its incidence may be less severe, mainly because people are often less durable and more mobile than property. Thus, professional licensing—whether of doctors, nurses, teachers, chiropodists, beauticians, barbers, or plumbers–tends to create implicit grants toward these professions. The restrictive practices of medical associations undoubtedly increase the incomes of doctors beyond what they would be if these restrictions did not exist. It is claimed, of course, that these restrictions are necessary in order to protect the public from unqualified practitioners, and there is something in this claim. However, the temptation to extend these restrictions beyond what is strictly necessary to protect the public seems to be almost irresistible, and an implicit grants structure inevitably develops.

A solution that has been recommended for this problem, although it is not of universal applicability, is that where licensing is regarded as socially necessary, the licenses should be sold by auction, in which case the value of the implicit grants that are involved in licenses would be captured by the government, and hence their incidence would be distributed broadly over society at large. This means that the government would lose much of its control over who gets the licenses and that the licenses could no longer be used as an instrument of political power and political control. For those who are suspicious of political control over persons, this would be an advantage rather than a disadvantage. It is also claimed that a system of the sale of licenses would mean that only the rich would be able to get them. This, however, is a fallacy. It is only those who are best able to use them who would be able to get them. While certain defects of the financial system might prevent those who could well use the licenses from bidding for them because of the absence of credit facilities, this is, as it were, another part of the forest, for the problem of justice and democratization in credit is something that has to be treated separately.

IMPLICIT GRANTS IN CREDIT AND FINANCE

The implicit grants structure in the system of credit and finance is a problem of great interest that has received little attention. There may be a system of informal quotas and licenses in both private and public banking systems that favors one set of potential customers at the expense of another. Financial markets are so imperfect simply because the commodities in which they deal, such as trustworthiness, are so unstandardized that rationing bank loans is almost inevitable. A bank does not adjust the total volume of its loans by daily adjustments in its interest rates intended to scare off enough potential customers to the point where only the desired volume of loans is made. At existing loan rates in prosperous times there are usually more borrowers than the bank wants to accommodate, and in depression there may be fewer borrowers. In either case, however, the bank has to exercise discretion based on its judgment of the trustworthiness of the applicant, and this discretion easily leads into restriction. Rationing of this kind always leads to some sort of implicit grant, for those who have access to credit benefit in part, at any rate, at the expense of those who do not. The democratization of credit is perhaps one of the most remarkable phenomena in the last hundred years and has received too little attention, either in regard to its causes or its effects. We have seen an enormous increase in the proportion of the population that has access to credit of different kinds, the results of which are inevitably to diminish the implicit grants implied in the credit system. Nevertheless, implicit grants still remain, and because they are so hard to identify, it is very hard to do anything about them.[6]

A much neglected area of discussion in economics is the redistributional or implicit grants effects of both monetary and fiscal policy. By *monetary and fiscal policy* we generally mean those regulations or actions of government that are designed mainly to prevent unemployment or inflation, through operations that affect the quantity of money and debt or the composition and character of various kinds of money and debt. By *monetary policy* we usually mean those actions or regulations that operate primarily through the banking system and financial markets—for instance, changes in central bank rediscount rates, in the reserve requirements of other banks, or in direct open-market operations of a central bank by which it increases or diminishes the total quantity of the bank reserves and so affects the lending policies of the banking and financial system. By *fiscal policy* we generally mean those manipulations of the tax and expenditure structure of government—and also, to some extent, the manipulation of its debt structure—that will change the quantity of money and other fiscal assets in private hands. Thus, if the government runs a cash deficit (takes in less money than it pays out), this clearly results in an increase in the cash balances of the public. If it pays off debt, this diminishes government bonds in the hands of the public, and so on.

All these policies have been conceived usually in strictly aggregate terms, as instruments to increase or diminish aggregate demand. Nevertheless, it is impossible for any kind of policy to be implemented without there being some implicit grants effects, and these effects are rarely taken into consideration, partly because they are so difficult to trace. Just because a problem is difficult, however, does not mean that we should give up on it. The redistributive effects of fiscal policy depend very much, of course, on the specific form that either tax increases or reductions, or expenditure increases or reductions, actually take. Who pays increased taxes, and who is released from paying diminished taxes? Who receives increased expenditures, and who does not receive decreased expenditures? There is no general answer, of course, to these questions; one has to examine each specific case. Thus, the tax decrease of 1964 in the United States, which was very successful as far as overall fiscal policy is concerned, in that it helped to give us a decade of almost full employment, may very well have had a redistributive effect toward the rich. Even general tax relief frequently causes redistributions toward the rich because they usually pay more in taxes than the poor. Where the tax relief is in the form of concessions to business, or a decline in the progressivity of the tax system, the implicit grants to the rich may be larger. Also on the expenditure side, public works frequently benefit the rich more than the poor. Subsidies for superhighways, for instance, are a grant to those who have automobiles, and even if 80 percent of the people have automabiles, this still means an implicit grant toward them and away from the 20 percent who do not, who are generally in the poorer end of the income spectrum.

Thus, fiscal policy as a means of achieving stable full employment must also be examined in the light of its implicit redistributions. Cash budget deficits in government, for instance, have a direct effect in increasing the amount of money in the possession of the public, but the question, Which public? is very seldom asked. The distribution of the increased money stocks in the first instance is very rarely uniform, and even the macroeconomic effects of these increased stocks are going to depend in no small measure on who gets them. If they go mainly to the rich, for instance, through tax relief at higher levels and so on, the effects are going to be very different from what they would be if they went to the poor.

The distributional effects of so-called monetary policy have received even less consideration.[7] The object of these policies is usually to make borrowing easier and cheaper in times of depression and more difficult and more expensive in times of inflation. The main macroeconomic impact, therefore, is on investment rather than on consumption, although consumption may be affected by household loans, mortgage loans, other forms of consumer credit, and changes in the quantity and distribution of the money stock. The redistributional effects of these measures are usually unknown, but they cannot be assumed to be insignificant. Just as it is the richer part of the population that uses highways, so is it the richer part that uses credit. Hence, easier credit conditions may easily operate as a subsidy to the richer part of the population, although it may also make it possible, for local governments especially, to borrow for purposes that in fact subsidize the poor. Similarly, while there is a certain presumption that tighter credit conditions may affect the rich more adversely than the poor, it is not a foregone conclusion, and it may, for instance, simply lead to redistributions among the rich. The redistributive effects of higher interest rates are almost totally unknown. A rise in interest rates redistributes income from the people who pay interest to the people who receive it, but whether the people who pay interest are richer or poorer than the people who receive it, we simply do not know.

REDISTRIBUTIVE EFFECTS OF INFLATION, PRICE CONTROL, AND PUBLIC INVESTMENT

Similar problems are involved when considering the redistributive effects of inflation. One study[8] has suggested that inflation is not much of a burden on the poor, certainly by comparison with deflation and unemployment, which redistribute income away from the poor toward the less poor. We really do not know, however, who pays for inflation. It is obvious that inflation must have a considerable redistributive implicit grants effect. It injures pensioners and people with fixed incomes, sticky incomes, and contractual incomes and benefits the profit maker and those who are in good bargaining positions. Outside of these very broad principles we know very little about how inflation redistributes income. There is some evidence, for instance, that in inflationary periods the wages of unorganized labor rise faster than the wages of organized labor. This conclusion may seem surprising at first. However, it follows because one of the major effects of trade unionism and labor organization is to make the fixing of wages a time-consuming process, so that in an inflationary period the sheer time involved in the wage negotiations of organized labor creates a lag, despite some cost-of-living clauses in contracts. By contrast, the rapid bargains of the unorganized labor market catch up with the inflation very easily. The opposite effect occurs in deflation, when organized wages stay up and unorganized wages decline sharply. We know, also, that inflation tends to shift income away from interest receivers toward profit receivers. Again, we do not really know whether interest receivers are poorer or richer than profit receivers.

A similar fog of ignorance surrounds the distributional effects of wage, price, and rent control. As we have noted, almost the only administratively feasible procedure in these matters is to freeze a set of wages, prices, or rents as they are listed on a given date and then set up an administrative apparatus to adjust the relative structures when these become obsolete, either for reasons of changes in productivity or out of some sense of injustice in redistribution. It has universally been found that this administrative machinery never catches up with the high rate of obsolescence of any given relative wage, price, or rent structure. On the production and consumption side we tend to get shortages and surpluses. Commodities whose prices are fixed relatively too low tend to disappear from the market. Housing under rent control, where rents are too low, is simply not provided and allowed to depreciate, and new private housing is not built. If wages are fixed too low in a particular occupation, a severe labor shortage may develop, and all these things create pressure for administrative change. Administrative change, however, is much slower in response to these feedbacks than is change in the market system. The usual pattern is for the strains to accumulate to the point where the whole system breaks down and has to be abandoned, or dissolves in black markets.

Here again, the distributional aspects of these policies have rarely been studied and little is really known about them. It is quite possible, for instance, that under some circumstances landlords may be poorer than renters, so that rent control, which forces rents down, creates an implicit grant from the poorer landlords to the richer renters. In the first two periods of wage and price control that the United States has experienced since 1940, during World War II and the Korean War, there does seem to have been a shift in the distribution of national income away from profits toward wages, suggesting perhaps that price control is easier than wage control.

Other areas in which implicit grants have been almost entirely neglected are in conservation and environmental policies and in public investments in such things as water projects, flood control, irrigation projects, harbors, roads, bridges—all of which are designed presumably to alter the environment in favor of man. The standard that is usually applied to justify these investments in structural alterations is that of cost-benefit analysis—an attempt to assess in monetary terms the total costs and total benefits of a project. Even though this is frequently a rather ritualistic procedure designed to justify a decision taken before the analysis, it is certainly better to have some cost-benefit analysis rather than none.

On the other hand, the distribution of the costs and benefits is almost universally neglected. For example, the fact that the benefits may be received by a quite different set of people from those who pay the costs is rarely taken into consideration. There is a strong presumption that the benefits of environmental and developmental projects of all kinds are likely to go to the richer part of the population, and costs are all too frequently paid by the poor simply because of their political weakness. Thus, the benefits even in such virtuous public projects as the Tennessee Valley Authority (TVA), the National Park System, the Soil Conservation Service, the Bureau of Reclamation, and the Army Corps of Engineers frequently accrue to the richer part of the population. Poor people do not enjoy national parks, camp in the national forests, sail their boats on the lakes produced by the TVA or by the Army Corps of Engineers; and even the people who are protected by flood control schemes are likely to be the property owners who have had the poor wisdom to build in flood plains. Poor people may not be directly injured by these projects and, so far as the tax system is progressive, may not be injured at all by them. The redistributions may be among the richer part of the population. The possibility that the poor may suffer from these otherwise virtuous projects is rarely, if ever, taken into consideration, and these questions should always be raised.

If this chapter has sounded depressingly like a catalog of ignorance, this unfortunately reflects the state of the art. It is again perhaps a reflection of the fact that economics has been obsessed by exchange and has failed to recognize the significance of the grants element in the economy, so that the theory of incidence—which is what we have really been talking about in this chapter—has been largely confined to those explicit public grants made through the tax system. The fact that exactly the same problem of incidence arises in any public policy has been shockingly neglected.

NOTES

1. External economies are said to occur even in the absence of technical change when the expansion of one industry lowers the cost of another. The concept can easily be extended to include technical change if technical change in one industry induces cost-lowering technical change in another.

2. See K. E. Boulding, *Economic Analysis*, 4th ed. (New York: Harper & Row, 1966), pp. 207–17.

3. The *short run* can be defined as that period within which the adjustments that are eventually going to be made have not yet been made. The *long run* is that period in which the adjustments that are going to be made have been made.

4. Viscount Astor and B. S. Rountree, *British Agriculture* (London: Longmans, 1938), p. 219.

5. Don Paarlberg, *American Farm Policy* (New York: John Wiley & Sons, 1964), chap. 25.

6. See Kenneth E. Boulding and Thomas F. Wilson, eds., *Redistribution through the Financial System: The Grants Economics of Money and Credit* (New York: Praeger, 1978).

7. The terminology used among economists at this point may cause confusion among the laymen, as it is *fiscal* policy that in the case of cash deficits operates most directly on the quantity of money in the hands of the public, whereas *monetary* policy operates mainly on conditions in financial and security markets and only indirectly on the quantity of money and its distribution.

8. See Robert G. Hollister and John L. Palmer, "The Impact of Inflation on the Poor," in *Redistribution to the Rich and the Poor*, ed. Kenneth E. Boulding and Martin Pfaff (Belmont, Calif.: Wadsworth, 1972).

5

The Theory of
Exploitation

THE MEANINGS OF EXPLOITATION

We now come to what is perhaps the most difficult and controversial aspect of the grants economy—the problem of the legitimacy of grants, either explicit or implicit. Intimately connected with this problem is an argument about what are grants and what are not. The argument also extends to the question of the legitimacy of exchange, which cannot really be separated from the legitimacy of grants, since exchange and grants are alternative methods of organizing society. The question of the proper boundary between the exchange economy and the grants economy lies at the root of a great deal of political and economic controversy.

Exploitation is a word that frequently has much more emotive than intellectual content. The exploitation of humans by humans is universally recognized to be a bad thing. There is a neutral use of the word, in the sense of the exploitation of opportunities or resources, although the pejorative meaning often even extends to this use. I recall the old joke about capitalism being a system in which man exploits man, whereas under socialism the reverse is the case. However, despite the fact that the word is used in a loose and rhetorical manner, it clearly corresponds to some phenomenon in the real world, and it is important to try to put clear intellectual content into it, so that we can at least hope to distinguish exploitation from nonexploitation or even one kind of exploitation from another. Bad categories leading to the failure of perceptual discrimination is perhaps the most important single source of bad politics.

I propose, therefore, a working definition of exploitation, as a grant or one-way transfer of an exchangeable, whether explicit or implicit, that is regarded by the grantor at least as illegitimate. I have used this definition rather than the narrower one of grants made under coercion or under threat, even though coercion is a very significant source of the sense of illegitimacy, because not all grants made under threat are regarded as illegitimate. Thus, taxes collected by a government widely considered legitimate by the taxpayers are in some sense collected under threat. That is, they are coerced grants. Taxes are admitted as legitimate, however, because this seems to be the only answer to what economists call the freeloader principle.[1] As W. J. Baumol has pointed out, it is quite rational for people to vote to coerce themselves if everybody else is likewise coerced.[2] If governments were supported by purely voluntary contributions, it is highly likely that they would not be supported very well, and the whole society would suffer from insufficient public goods. It is not the element of threat or coercion alone, therefore, that creates a sense of exploitation but the feeling of illegitimacy. The taxpayer does not necessarily feel that he is exploited by a government he regards as legitimate, but any taxes collected by a government regarded as illegitimate can be regarded as exploitation.

Some may regard this definition as unsatisfactory because it is not "objective," for legitimacy is an essentially subjective phenomenon. The same objective transfer can be regarded as legitimate under some circumstances and as illegitimate under others. I can only defend the definition by saying that this is what I think the world is like and that no matter how subjective legitimacy is and how uncertain and difficult it is to discover the principles governing the dynamics of legitimacy, nevertheless, it is this concept that is significant. There is no point in developing easy concepts that are not true. We see this even in the extreme case of such obvious exploitation as slavery, which in the modern world is rightly regarded with abhorrence as a totally illegitimate form of human relationship. We would now find almost universal agreement that slaves are exploited in that they produce more than their maintenance and in that this surplus does not go to them but to their masters, and their masters give them nothing in return. Because of the power of their threat capability, masters are able to say to the slave in effect, "You work for me for mere maintenance or I will kill you." Then if the slave produces more than his maintenance, he makes in effect a grant to the master that is not wholly unlike the grant that a victim makes to a bandit.

Slaveholders, however, have argued that it is more like the grant a taxpayer pays to his government. Where slavery is recognized as legitimate—and there have been societies in which both the slaves and the slaveholders have regarded slavery as legitimate or have simply not raised the question—then the slave is paying taxes in kind to a legitimate authority, his master. These implicit taxes are presumably paid for the public good of living in the society at all, just as a citizen pays taxes to his government without exploitation. Thus, the same objective situation of slavery and the same objective transfers may be regarded as exploitation under one view of legitimacy and not as exploitation under another, even though we may rightly regard the latter view as illegimate. We cannot avoid recognizing the overwhelming importance of the structure of legitimacy in any definition of exploitation.

In general, we can say that whether there is an attitude that identifies certain relations and transactions as illegitimate depends a great deal on the legitimacy or acceptance of the existing structure of terms of trade. The slave is an extreme case of terms of trade that are regarded as too poor to be legitimate. We see the same phenonenon in a milder way in the feeling that farmers have had almost universally that the terms of trade of agriculture are too poor and hence involve some kind of exploitation. As the old song goes, "The farmer comes to town with his wagon broken down, but the farmer is the man that feeds them all." Farmers have constantly felt that they were exploited in that their output of foodstuffs, without which the society could not exist, is rewarded with an inadequate return in other commodities. This sense of illegitimacy can become particularly strong when the farmer sees a considerable part of his produce going to support landlords, who seem to give him very little in return. It is not surprising that the payment of rent is often seen as something exploitative—a grant from the poor farmer to the rich landlord. Payments of interest also often seem to the payer to be a grant to the lender, which may be regarded as illegitimate. The medieval prejudice against usury and the extraordinary intellectual acrobatics used by medieval schoolmen to distinguish legitimate interest from illegitimate interest are good examples of the principle that what is perceived as an illegitimate grant is also perceived as exploitation.

THE MARXIST CONCEPT

We cannot discuss exploitation much further without referring to the work of Karl Marx, whose significance lies mainly in the fact that he systematized the concept and thereby profoundly affected the processes of legitimation and delegitimation. Marx crystallized into a system the rather incoherent feelings about exploitation that people had had a very long time. The instrument with which Marx achieved this remarkable result was the labor-embodied theory of value. This theory held that the value of a commodity is measured by the quantity of labor embodied in it—that is, the labor that has gone to making it in circumstances that can be written as normal or, in Marxist terms, "socially necessary." Adam Smith and David Ricardo originally designed this theory for totally different purposes, mainly as a first approximation theory of the determinants of an equilibrium structure of relative prices. If I were to explain to an intelligent child why an automobile is worth in the market about 10,000 loaves of bread, it is at least not a bad first approximation to say that it takes about 10,000 times as much labor to make an automobile as it does to make a loaf of bread.

In the hands of Marx, however, the labor theory became a theory of exploitation. His theory can be summarized very simply by saying that labor produces everything, but labor does not receive all that it produces because some of the product goes to the owners of property—landlords and capitalists. Marx regarded this as an illegitimate grant from the working class to the property owners, which is made as a result of the power structure of capitalist society. Property owners control the organized internal threat system of society and hence control those governmental processes that protect and perpetuate a system of private property. They are thus able to prevent the working class from using government to transfer to themselves the products that the property-owning class enjoys.

We cannot go into this subtle and complex argument here in any great detail; enough has been written about it elsewhere. However, it should be noted that Marx regarded the exchange economy, under conditions of private ownership of property in the physical means of production, as producing a wage and price structure that creates an illegitimate transfer of surplus value from the working class to the property owners. The surplus value may be defined roughly as the difference between what the working class produces and what it receives in wages. The actual theoretical model Marx used was such an extremely special case that it has rarely had applicability in the real world, although there are societies for which it makes sense as a first approximation. In Marx's system wages are determined by a subsistence-level model that he took rather uncritically from the classical economists (the subsistence level being that level of real wages at which the working class is just able and willing to subsist and to reproduce itself). As the accumulation of capital increases productivity, the total product of the society rises in per capita terms, but real wages do not because of the superior bargaining power of the capitalist class. Hence, the proportion of the total product that goes to property owners continually increases, eventually bringing the system down in ruins through depressions of ever-increasing intensity.

The actual dynamics of the successful capitalist countries have been very different. The proportion of wages in national income has tended to increase rather than to diminish. In the United States, for instance, it was probably less than 50 percent in the nineteenth century; it is 75 percent today, and any subsistence theory of wages is obviously nonsense. Marx's subsistence theory of wages, indeed, implies a degree of monopoly power on the part of capitalists that they do not usually have, except in the very unusual case of slave societies, or perhaps in the case of large landed estates and peonage. Consequently, the very operations of the market economy and the competition of capitalists for labor in a society in which productivity is increasing and per capita incomes are increasing force wages up, even to the point that the actual proportion of national income going to labor increases. The actual mechanism behind this process is complex, and by no means is there agreement among economists about it. The facts, however, are indisputable, and whatever the possible virtues of the Marxist analysis it must be regarded as an extremely special case.

Nevertheless, even if it does not give the right answers, the Marxist analysis raises some important questions that remain astonishingly persistent, so that all the efforts of "bourgeois" economists, from Nassau Senior[3] to E. Von Böhm-Bawerk[4] to Milton Friedman,[5] have not quite made the questions go away. We may have our foot on the head of the Marxist dragon, but it still manages to breathe a certain amount of smoke and fire.

GRANTS ELEMENTS IN PROFIT AND INTEREST

The relevant question for our discussion is whether there is a grants element in incomes derived from nonhuman property—that is, profit, interest, and rent. Even from the narrow point of view of the accounting concepts we use to differentiate grants from exchange (grants being relationships in which there is redistribution of net worth), interest and profit have a somewhat ambiguous status. The accounting conventions really imply that exchange is of equal value, whether in trade or in production. Thus, from the firm's point of view, the purchase of $100 worth of raw materials is entered in the books as a diminution of $100 on the cash side and an increase of $100 on the raw materials side. This is the essence of double-entry bookkeeping. Similarly, with the principle of valuation of stocks or inventory at cost (neglecting the "cost or market, whichever is the lower" of traditional accounting, and the "FIFO-LIFO" controversy),[6] the inference is that a given quantity of finished product is valued at the dollar value of other assets that have been sacrificed in order to produce it. If $100 worth of raw material, $200 worth of labor, and $100 worth of depreciation of fixed plant and machinery have been involved in the production of a given amount of finished product, it is valued conventionally at $400. Profit emerges in the process of revaluation of assets rather than in exchange, although the revaluation and the exchange often take place simultaneously. Thus, our $400 worth of finished product may now be sold for $500, in which case the firm increases its net worth by $100. This can be broken down hypothetically into a revaluation at the moment of sale of the finished product, from $400 to $500, and then its exchange for an equal value in money.

The origin of profit in revaluation gives some plausibility to the Marxist contention that if exchange is of equal values, how can profit arise without some sort of exploitation? That is, the revaluations, which really constitute profit, look like a grant in that they seem to represent at least an increase in the net worth of one party. The critical question is, Do they represent a decrease in the net worth of some other party? If they do, then Marx was right; profit is a grant, not something that arises out of exchange. Under some circumstances it might be argued that we could identify the parties who lose net worth as a result of a profit maker gaining it. In general, however, it is virtually impossible to do this, not only because of the general difficulty of the theory of incidence and of finding the real patterns of the implicit grants network but also because in many cases what has happened in the profit-making process is not just a redistribution of net worths but a creation of net worths. That is, the revaluation of the finished product when it is sold represents a net addition to the total net worth of the society, which is a contribution of the profit-making process by which the owners of capital exchange assets and rearrange them in the course of the processes of production.

If now we believe in a pure labor theory of value, or what might better be called the labor theory of the total product, then we have to deny the productivity of the ownership of capital. That is, we have to deny that the capitalist, through the kind of ownership or control that he has, can increase the product of society through his activities. Indeed, Marx argued that there was a kind of "labor of management" that contributed to the product like any other labor. However, he denied that the institution of private ownership contributed to the product, and this indeed is the heart of the controversy. If we regard the total product as produced mechanically by the aggregation of specific acts of labor, obviously ownership as such has no role, although management may have a part to play.

We saw earlier that the definition of an implicit grant structure always rests on some concept of a norm from which the existing system of distribution of welfare is a divergence. The real issue in the Marxist controversy, therefore, is whether there are other forms of social organization that are as productive as the system of organization based on private property. This question cannot really be answered a priori; in fact, it may not be capable of any definitive answer simply because we do not know all the alternative forms of social organization. We certainly cannot rule out the possibility that some social invention or mutation yet to come could in fact be more productive in some acceptable sense of the word than an organization based on private property. At the moment, however, the case against private property, at least in some limited and controlled form, must be regarded as "not proven," in the words of the old Scottish verdict. At the moment a whole spectrum of types of organization of society is developing. The ideal types of pure capitalism, based on the bare minimum of government designed to provide limited public goods and security of private property, and pure socialism, based on the government ownership and operation of all economic resources, are really empty boxes with no real-world examples to be found in them. Instead we have a great variety of intermediate states, which are in fact quite difficult to classify along this simple spectrum. In many ways, for instance, capitalist West Germany is more like Communist East Germany than either West Germany is like the United States or East Germany is like the Soviet Union.[7]

COMPARISONS OF SOCIALISM AND CAPITALISM

The critical question is, of course, What do we mean by the productivity of institutions? We have to answer this question in dynamic terms. One test is whether the institutions produce real economic growth. This is not necessarily the same thing as increase in per capita GNP, although the growth in per capita GNP is at least a place to start from in trying to measure the realities of true net growth in welfare. As some countries with a high degree of capitalism and other countries with a high degree of socialism have all experienced economic growth, it is clear that the evaluation of economic and social institutions by this criterion may well be very ambiguous. Our evaluations may depend much more on criteria that do not get into economic statistics than those that do. In terms of equality and distribution of real incomes, especially of the real economic welfare of households, the free market societies, and what might be called the business socialist societies, such as the Soviet Union and Eastern Europe, and even North Korea, are not strikingly different, given their different levels of development. In some ways the equality of incomes depends more on the nature of the product mix and of the technology of the society than it does on its formal institutions or even on its grants economy. A society of almost universal automobiles, mass-produced clothing, developed agriculture with plentiful foodstuffs, and mass-produced housing is almost inevitably egalitarian as compared with a society in earlier stages of development, in which only a very small proportion of the society can even be middle class.

In terms of consumer goods it is quite likely that the socialist countries are less egalitarian than the capitalist countries simply because the capitalist countries are on the whole richer. Most socialist countries are still in the stage where an automobile, for instance, is a privilege of the few. The housing that has been built in the twentieth century in both capitalist and socialist countries is clearly egalitarian. We now build apartment houses or vast suburbs instead of palaces, and it is likely that both socialist and capitalist countries at the same level have about the same proportion of people in what might be called substandard housing and substandard environments.

Historically, the whole argument between capitalism and socialism, at least of the conventional kinds, seems to have ended in a draw, and the reason for this is that the labor theory of value is just simply wrong. The product is produced not merely by acts of labor but by an enormous interaction of persons in the communication system, some of which may be organized by private property and private exchange and some by a public grants economy. Indeed, it is by no means absurd to stand Marx on his head and develop a capital theory of value, arguing that labor produces nothing, just as raw materials in the ground produce nothing. It is the process of organization by which labor is hired, employed, and directed, by which raw materials are brought together, by which machinery and buildings are assembled, by which processes of production are organized, that in fact creates the product; labor by itself is an inert mass incapable of producing little more than scratching a meager living from the woods. The organizer who really creates the product, however, almost has to be either an owner or a controller of property.

In socialist and capitalist countries alike we get the spectacle of the famous "separation of ownership from control,"[8] which seems to be necessary if processes of production are to be organized, if only because those who own are seldom very good at controlling, and those who are good at controlling seldom have ownership. In capitalist societies this organization is achieved through the operations of the financial markets, through such instrumentalities as debt, bonds, and stocks. A good manager or a good organization of managers can control a much larger quantity of assets than they themselves own—by borrowing money, by issuing bonds, or by issuing stock. Stockholders have some claims to ultimate control of the enterprise, but it is well known that these claims are rarely exercised and that most enterprises are run by a self-perpetuating group of managers. Things are not very different in the socialist countries. The people as a whole are supposed to own the equity in the physical capital of the society, but they do not usually even have the formal rights of the stockholder. There is frequently widespread discussion of the economic plan, but the ultimate decisions rest with a very small group of managers, and the theoretical ownership of the people results in remarkably little control. The component organizations of the two types of society also exhibit many similarities. In its organizational structure, and even in many of its decision-making processes, the Soviet steel trust is not very different from the United States Steel Corporation, and it is hardly different at all from corporations like Lockheed or Martin Aircraft, which derive almost all their revenue and a great deal of their capital from the U.S. government.

The essential difference between the two types of society—and this will be significant even in distinguishing between, say, Sweden as one of the more socialist of the capitalist countries and Yugoslavia as one of the more capitalist of the "socialist camp" countries—lies in the existence or nonexistence of a private capital market, which again goes back to the question of the legitimacy in the society of this form of exchange and organization. The capitalist corporation can expand if it is successful in making profits—that is, if it can revalue its products successfully at the moment of sale so that the returns are above costs. It can expand either by not distributing its profits or by going into the capital market and selling stocks, bonds, or promissory notes. By any of these means it can expand the total volume of assets over which it has control. A socialist trust likewise, if it wishes to expand, has to go into the socialist equivalent of the capital market—the government agency that disburses investment funds.

What is badly needed in this controversy is some kind of cost-benefit analysis of the alternative systems, and although it may not be possible to do this in a way that would resolve the controversy, at least some movement in this direction would be fruitful. There are many elements in each system on which it is hard to put a valuation, and there may be disagreement about the elements of the systems themselves. But if the questions can be taken out of the sphere of ideological controversy into that of sober analysis, we would at least have greater insight into what the controversy is about. A system analysis would also point to the places where an improvement in the data would improve our capacity to evaluate the two systems. A tentative analysis might be put in tabular form as follows:

Costs

Capital Markets	*Central Planning*
1. We could measure the proportion of the GNP absorbed by the financial system. This would include employees of banks, insurance companies, financial houses, the stock markets, and so on, plus the real resources absorbed in their buildings and capital equipment.	1. In the socialist country we could measure the proportion of the GNP absorbed by the central planning bureau, its employees, its capital equipment, and so on, plus some proportion of real resources absorbed in a system of public finance and in the state banking systems.

2. That part of net national product or national income absorbed by the owners of capital in their own consumption may in the short run at least be regarded as a cost to the rest of society; if the property owners did not consume these goods, they would be available for the rest of the people. It seems to be impossible to have a capital market without creating a class of people who live off the income from capital. There are offsets to this, however, as we shall see.

2. Income from interest on state bonds is a fairly common feature of socialist societies, although it is much smaller usually than in capitalist societies. There is, however, a certain tendency for party members and government officials to get benefits, often in kind, such as the use of automobiles, bigger houses, and so on, which also may withdraw resources from the rest of the society.

Benefits

Capital Markets

Central Planning

3. It is much more difficult to assess the benefits than it is the costs. These are, however, quite real. Capital markets exhibit great flexibility. People with a bright idea and a certain gift of persuasion, if they can establish their credibility, can obtain funds and resources to bring their idea to fruition. Capital markets also permit a fair degree of consumer sovereignty in that people who produce something that consumers do not want are not likely to be successful, and those who produce what people want will have success. The feedback from the market is not always as rapid as might be desired, but it undoubtedly exists. There is nothing in the capital market either that precludes it from organizing a supply to satisfy a demand for public goods as well

3. Investment in the socialist societies is supposed to be in the interest of the whole society, but there is actually very little feedback from the decisions that are made and no very good criterion to judge when these decisions have been wrong. Consequently, there is a strong presumption that the benefits of investment are less than they would be if there was the kind of information system that a capital market provides, or some substitute for this.

as private goods. Agencies of government with the right to borrow in financial markets have great advantage when it comes to flexibility over those that have to rely on rigid budgets.

4. The dynamics of the distribution of income and wealth in capitalist societies are not easy to identify and are still harder to evaluate. Nevertheless, the distribution of income at any one time depends on the distribution of property, including the property in minds and bodies, and may depend also on the grants matrix, both explicit and implicit. The distribution, between, say, labor income and property income is not the same thing as the distribution of income by size. Not all capitalists are rich and not all laborers are poor, and, indeed, property income may in part represent a transfer from rich plumbers, or even richer executives, to poor widows. It may also represent a transfer from poor migrant workers to rich landowners, and this grants matrix needs to be known before it can be evaluated. The long-run dynamics of the distribution of property depend very much on the technology of the system: its inheritance laws, marriage customs, and a large number of other variables. There may be some tendency for capital markets to lead to greater concentration of wealth, on the famous principle that "to him that hath

4. Socialist societies exhibit varying degrees of egalitarianism .There is a real difference in this respect between the business socialism of the Soviet Union and Eastern Europe, which has developed wide inequalities of income mainly in the interest of increased output, and the radical egalitarian societies of Cuba and Maoist China. In all socialist societies, however, there is very extreme concentration of power, which is an inevitable consequence of the destruction of consumer sovereignty and capital markets . This concentration of power in the hands of central planners always seems to involve the danger of tyranny—that is, a society organized by fear or a monopoly of persuasion rather than by consent, which is reflected in large expenditures on secret police, purges, the absence of a free press, restrictions on intellectual life, and so on. Whether these are necessary concomitants of social-ism is hard to say. That they are probable concomitants seems hard to deny in the light of the historical record of the twentieth century.

shall be given," for the rich find it easier to save and add to their riches than do the poor. On the other hand, there are many offsets of this principle, such as the extravagance of heirs and the propensity of particular capitalists to lose their money. Both inflation and deflation destroy old propertied classes. Inflation destroys the renter and the landlord; deflation destroys the profit maker. Thus, many aspects of capital markets promote the circulation of elites as well as the maintenance of family fortunes.

5. The role of persuasion in a society must be included in any evalua - tion, yet again it is hard to identify and evaluate. Some critics of capi - talist society, such as Kenneth Galbraith,[9] have suggested that persuasion, especially on the part of producers and government, seriously undermines consumer sovereignty. Galbraith argues, for instance, that what he calls the "accepted sequence" by which producers are supposed to follow the demands of consumers and by which governments are supposed to follow the demands of voters is in fact seriously modified by the "revised sequence," according to which producers decide what they want to produce and then persuade the consumers through all the powers of advertising to demand what the producers have decided to produce. Governments, likewise, decide what they want to do and

5. On the socialist side the revised sequence is of dominating importace. There is no pretense of consumer sovereignty or of voter sovereignty, and in the absence of a market the only alternatives seem to be fear or persuasion as social organizers. It is not surprising, therefore, that a great deal of effort is devoted in social - ist societies to persuasion. Chairman Mao's "Little Red Book" was an example of the revised sequence, which would make any disciple of Madison Avenue green with envy. Chairman Mao decided what was good for China and then brought into being an enormous apparatus to persuade people that he was right. The collapse of Maoism in China, however, suggests that even a total monopoly of persua - sion cannot persuade people indefinitely to believe things that are not true. Even Maoist China

THEORY OF EXPLOITATION / 95

then persuade the electorate that this is really what they want. The existence of these revised sequences can hardly be doubted. On the other hand, their failure is quite frequent. It is hard to estimate their quantitative importance.

could not fool all of the people all of the time!

6. A miscellaneous group of items can be regarded either as costs or benefits, depending on whether we evaluate them negatively or positively. Consumer sovereignty may easily lead into vulgarity, for ordinary people often fail to operate by the austere standards regarded as desirable by political puritans. One could make out a case, however, for having a class of rich people on the grounds that they will pioneer in matters of taste, culture, life-styles, and commodity mixes. It is not unreasonable to suppose that there is a degree of inequality that will optimize the quality of life of the whole society. Where this lies is difficult to evaluate. Lively development of the arts, especially in poorer societies, may require the concentration of a certain amount of surplus value into a small group.

6. Socialist societies exhibit a certain drabness and uniformity. The concentration of power can easily lead to corruption of the arts, as it did in the Soviet Union, or even corruption in the sciences, as in the famous Lysenko case. On the other side, there is the development of a strong sense of national community in socialist societies that gives purpose and significance to individual life—a sense often missing in the looser vulgarities of capitalism. The differences of different people in the evaluation of these elements may easily make the crucial difference in their ultimate preferences between the two types of society.

PROFIT AS EXCHANGE: A REWARD FOR "WAITING"

We should not conclude this chapter without a brief look at the arguments that have been used by classical and neoclassical economists to bring income derived from capital—that is, profit and interest—within the general framework of the exchange economy. The critical question is whether interest and profit are paid "for something"—that is, whether they are part of an exchange relationship or whether they are a grant or one-way transfer, as the Marxists suggest. The first prominent economist to pay much attention to this problem was Nassau Senior, who argued that income from capital was paid for something called "abstinence."[10] Capital was acquired in the individual case by saving—consuming less than one's income. Sometimes this can be regarded as abstaining from dissaving; that is, consuming capital—by consuming more than one's income. If capital is to be accumulated, it is clear that the society as a whole must have abstinence in this sense, and the problem of how to prevent consumption rising until it absorbs the whole product, or even more than the whole product, is a real one, especially in poor societies. Interest and profit, then, are regarded as rewards for what is a perfectly real activity (that of not consuming as much as one's income), even if it is a negative one. It is argued that if the rate of interest and profit were zero, there would be no incentive to abstain from consuming as much as one's income, or indeed from consuming one's capital, and society would decay. The rate of saving or accumulation is then seen as a function of the rate of return on capital, and as the accumulation of capital increases the capacity to create incomes in the future, what the rest of society receives from the capitalist receivers of interest and profit is the expectation of greater incomes in the future. It is interesting to see how many of the ideas of subsequent writers are really implicit in the work of Senior.

The next economist who devoted himself extensively to this problem was E. Von Böhm-Bawerk,[11] who had the advantage of writing after the Marxian criticism and was, indeed, a sharp critic of Marx.[12] Böhm-Bawerk envisaged physical capital as a population of goods, a good being born when it was produced and dying when it was consumed. Growth in the structure of capital increased the productivity of society, but this meant that the "average period of production"—that is, the average time interval between the birth and death of goods—had to increase and production had to become more "roundabout." Here again, interest and profit had to be paid to people to persuade them not to diminish but to increase their capital by postponing consumption and, therefore, enabling goods to exist longer and permit the establishment of those longer and more productive processes of production. The weakness of Böhm-Bawerk's theory was the absence of any dynamic element; his theory is essentially a comparative statics of stationary states and hence only throws a rather dim light on the dynamic realities of the world. Still, in a field as difficult as this, even a dim light has some value.

Alfred Marshall elaborated on Senior, using the expression *waiting* rather than *abstinence* as more neutral, but essentially the same thing.[13] Irving Fisher clarified the work of Böhm-Bawerk in what is still the definitive neoclassical work in this field.[14] In his great book on the theory of interest, he sees interest essentially as a property of exchanges over time. A gives B something valued at $x now, and B gives A something valued at $y, t years later. If there is a rate of interest or a rate of return, y will be larger than x, and the rate of return, r, is given by the formula $y = x (1 + r)^t$, assuming annual compounding. The promise to pay $y t years from now is a "security," and x is its price. It is clear that the larger x, the smaller will be the rate of return r. The problem of interest is, Why is not the price of securities so high that r is zero? In general the rate of return is that rate of growth of the present money payment for a security that will make this sum equal to the future net benefits or payments from the security. As Böhm-Bawerk saw very clearly, the answer to this question does not lie in any assumption about the productivity of physical capital as such, for no matter how productive capital might be, if its present value in the market were equal to its future product, the rate of return would still be zero. It is the evaluation in the present of expected future benefits that is the crux of the problem.

Irving Fisher saw this evaluation arising from a twofold set of properties of the market system, one on the demand side and one on the supply side. On the demand side the question is, Why does not the demand for securities, or any future expected benefits, push up their present price to the point where the rate of return is zero? The answer he suggested is that there is "impatience," that is, a preference for earlier as against later benefits of the same nominal size. To the question, Would you rather have $100 now, or $100 (of equal purchasing power) next year? most people would say, "$100 now." Then one could test the person's rate of time preference by asking, "Would you rather have $100 now or $101 next year?" "No!" "$110 next year?" "Maybe!" "$111 next year?" "Yes, I'll take it, not the $100 now!" The person's rate of time preference is then 11 percent per annum. This is a rate of time discount of future values. An interesting question is whether there is also a rate of uncertainty discount for future values, for the future usually becomes more uncertain the further we look into it.

Then on the supply side the question is, Why are people not willing to sell securities (promises of future benefits) at a price high enough so that there is a zero rate of return? The answer here seems to be that there is time productivity—that putting resources into employments that bear fruit only in the future gives more fruit than those that bear immediately. The growth of trees, of cattle, the maturing of wines are obvious examples of this principle, so much so that some writers, like Henry George, attributed all interest to such biological growth. However, there are also social growth processes that create time productivity—human and organizational learning and the time that it takes to get things put together and organized. It can be 10 to 20 years between the inception of a big engineering project and its completion, and perhaps 100 years of subsequent benefits, which could not take place without overcoming impatience. The capital market and the existence of positive rates of return and interest is one solution to this inescapable problem. Socialist societies have to solve the same problem, which they do essentially by forced saving and large grants, both explicit through taxation and implicit through the planned price structure, from workers and consumers to the investing state. Which solution is "better" is still a matter of acrimonious debate.

Marx and the Marxists have poked fun at the abstinence of the rich capitalists. With considerable justification Marx pointed to the phenomenon he called "primary accumulation"—that is, the concentration of productive resources into the hands of particular individuals through conquest, theft, extortion, marriage, and other nonmarket devices—and he argued that once capital had been concentrated in the hands of a few rich people, abstinence was very easy for them; whereas the abstinence of the poor was prohibitively costly and often meant sacrificing the real essentials of life. A man at the subsistence level cannot save (abstain from consumption) for any kind of reward at all. We might argue that some kind of primary accumulation is necessary to diminish the cost of abstinence and hence make capital accumulation and subsequent development possible. The communist countries, indeed, have gone in for primary accumulation—forced saving and forced transfers to the state—on a scale that far exceeds that of the capitalist societies.

The socialist countries have now come to recognize that a positive rate of return on capital, at least in the form of a rate of time preference, is necessary even in socialist accounting. Otherwise too much goes into investment, so that there is too much sacrifice in the present generation for the benefit of future generations, which is extremely difficult to justify in any principle of social justice. If the rate of interest, or at least the rate of time preference, is too low, there could also be too much investment in processes of production that take a long time to mature and not enough in short-period investments. This may easily lead to disastrous waste of investments in projects that cannot be carried to completion because of too great a commitment of investment resources in the past.

We can perhaps add another footnote to this long historical debate on capital theory by suggesting that one of the functions of the rate of return on capital is to prevent the exploitation of the present generation for the benefit of future generations, which has undoubtedly taken place in the socialist countries and may also take place in the capitalist countries in the early stages of accumulation. One has a certain sympathy with the man who asked, "What has posterity ever done for me?" A grant from the present generation to posterity could easily be regarded as exploitative of the present generation. The only case for grants of this kind is a sense of community over time, such as one gets in a family, in some corporate bodies, and, most strikingly, in a nation-state. One may get a certain present satisfaction in contemplating future national greatness.

It seems entirely legitimate, however, to discount the future not only for time but also for uncertainty. We run into this problem in the conservation of resources. How far should we abstain, for instance, in this generation from the consumption of fossil fuels (coal, oil, and gas) that are irreplaceable? Should we impose heavy extraction taxes to diminish present consumption in order that future generations may enjoy exhaustible resources longer? If we compare the value of a gallon of gasoline now with the value of a gallon of gasoline a hundred years from now, the gallon of gasoline a hundred years from now may be more valuable because gasoline then will be very scarce, but it will have to be a lot more valuable to justify the time discounting—that is, the impatience and uncertainty discounting—that we must do to compare it with a gallon now. One hundred years from now gaoline may not be used at all, for there may be other sources of power, now unknown.

The question of how much this generation should sacrifice for the benefit of its great-great-grandchildren, therefore, is by no means easy. These are questions that have to be faced in any kind of conservation policy, for it is difficult to say at what point we are exploiting our great-great-grandchildren and at what point they are exploiting us. On the other hand, the fact that we are alive and have votes, and they are not and do not have votes, makes posterity a pretty weak factor in the actual political decision-making process. Although they may curse us, their curses echo rather faintly from 100 years in the future. This means that there is a fairly strong presumption that we are exploiting them rather than they are exploiting us.

On the other hand, offsetting this gloomy view, there is the argument that the very history of development involves the exploitation of the present by the future generations. Our own inherited wealth, in the form of cities, roads, farms, works of art, and, above all, the great accumulated store of human knowledge, is the result of the "blood, sweat, and tears" of our ancestors, who produced more than they might have consumed, to our enormous benefit. The agonies of the pioneers, the anguish of the slaves, the enormous gifts of those who gave us our stock of literature, art, and science, often laboring for a minuscule reward, are testimony to the extent to which we have exploited the past. We, too, insofar as we are producing more than we consume, in buildings, capital goods of all kinds, and also in art, literature, and science, are contributing great grants to future generations. One hopes that with these two offsetting forces the exploitation of one generation by another, whether past or future, may not be so great after all.

NOTES

1. The freeloader principle describes the situation in which public goods, by nature available to everyone or to large numbers of people, have to be provided by some kind of specific economic activity. If there is no coercion, then anyone who does not contribute to the activity (the freeloader) can still enjoy the goods as long as other people (suckers) do contribute. The same principle applies to "public bads" such as pollution or exhaustion. This situation easily leads into what Garrett Hardin has called the "tragedy of the commons." See Garrett Hardin, *Exploring New Ethics for Survival: The Voyage of the Spaceship Beagle* (New York: Viking Press, 1972).

2. W. J. Baumol, *Welfare Economics and the Theory of the State* (Cambridge, Mass.: Harvard University Press, 1952). See also Mancur Olson, Jr., *The Logic of Collective Action* (Cambridge, Mass.: Harvard University Press, 1965).

3. Nassau W. Senior, *An Outline of the Science of Political Economy* (1836, reprint ed., New york: Kelley, 1965).

4. E. Von Böhm-Bawerk, *The Positive Theory of Capital*, trans. William Smart (Stechert, 1923).

5. Milton Friedman, *Capitalism and Freedom* (Chicago: University of Chicago Press, 1962).

6. FIFO, which stands for "first in, first out," and LIFO, which stands for "last in, first out," are alternative methods of estimating the value of inventory or goods in stock. See K. E. Boulding, *Economic Analysis*, 4th ed. vol. 1 (New York: Harper & Row, 1966) pp. 343–45.

7. F. L. Pryor, *Public Expenditures in Communist and Capitalist Nations* (Homewood, Ill.: Richard D. Irwin, 1968).

8. Adolph Berle and Gardiner Means, *The Modern Corporation and Private Property* (1932; rev. ed., New York: Harcourt Brace Jovanovich, 1969).

9. J. K. Galbraith, *The New Industrial State* (Boston: Houghton Mifflin, 1967).

10. Senior, *An Outline of the Science of Political Economy*. Two contemporaries of Senior, John Rae in Canada and Mountiford Longfield in Ireland, anticipated later theories of capital, but their contributions were not fully recognized until the end of the nineteenth century.

11. E. Von Böhm-Bawerk, *The Positive Theory of Capital*.

12. E. Von Böhm-Bawerk, *Karl Marx and the Close of His System* (London, 1896).

13. Alfred Marshall, *Principles of Economics*, 9th ed. (New York: Macmillan, 1961).

14. Irving Fisher, *The Theory of Interest* (Clifton, N.J.: Kelley, 1930).

6

The International Grants Economy

TRIBUTE AND AID

The international system, which includes transactions of all kinds that cross national boundaries, has always involved a complex mixture of exchange and grants. The international political system—that is, the direct relationships of states with each other—has relied extensively on threat as its major social organizer. This element of threat has frequently produced tribute in the form of indemnity payments after a lost war, such as the payments from France to Germany after 1871 or from Germany to the allies after World War I. Subsidies to allies, primarily for military purposes, have also been an important part of the international system almost from its beginnings. Grants from conquered peoples to their conquerors have also been a significant element in the international system. In the case of an empire it is hard to tell where a domestic system ends and an international system begins. The exploitation of slaves and peasants is as much a part of the domestic system as it is of the international system. Nevertheless, a rough distinction can be made between a domestic community, in which the people even if they are exploited have consciousness of belonging to a single nation or people, and an imperial relationship, in which the governed and the governors regard each other as aliens and not as part of the same national community.

In the twentieth century, and especially since the end of World War II, a new type of international transfer has grown up under the general heading of "foreign aid." To a considerable extent foreign aid is still part of the old system of payments to allies for military purposes, or payments to prevent resources from getting into the hands of an enemy, which has characterized the international system for so long. Part of it, however, is something different. It is a slowly growing recognition of the world community. A sharp world division between rich countries and poor countries not only may have elements of instability in it but also is morally uncomfortable for the rich. Something of the same rise in the sense of community or commensality, which gives rise to internal distributions within a country from the rich to the poor, can also be observed in the international system. This takes place even in the absence of a world government, except in the embryonic and possibly abortive form of the United Nations. Like other integrative grants, foreign aid may be motivated to some extent by considerations of prestige, a desire to have a favorable image in the world, or a desire to build up a national identity that is more satisfying to the nation's citizens. Nations, in their international relations, are so much more cruel, pitiless, selfish, and immoral than most persons in their personal relations that if the nation as an organization is not to lose the love and respect even of its own citizens, it has to create an aspect of its identity that is somewhat generous, philanthropic, and looking to the welfare of the human race. These motives are quite real in foreign aid, even though they are very much mixed in with motives of the more traditional strategic or threat-systems character.

WAR AS A "WASTE GRANT"

Because the international system operates so extensively at the level of threat and counterthreat, it becomes involved in arms races[1] and the building up of large defense industries, which involve very large internal public grants. The world war industry, as measured by military expenditures, is of the order of $400 billion, a little over a third of which is accounted for by the United States, somewhat under a third by the Soviet Union, and the rest by all the rest of the world. It is an often unrecognized paradox that the cost of maintaining a war industry is usually much greater than any actual damage to an enemy it causes. Even though a war industry is designed to produce "bads" rather than "goods," its most essential product, especially in an age of deterrence, is the threat to produce bads rather than the actual production of the bads themselves. Consequently, in peacetime the war industry directly produces very few bads, but its capability is achieved only at the sacrifice of goods that might otherwise have been produced. The $400 billion of the world war industry represents resources that could be employed in producing houses, schools, hospitals, roads, and and other commodities for the civilian population. In the United States, for instance, because of the rise in the war industry over the last 40 years, from under 1 percent of the economy in the 1930s to about 8 percent in the 1970s, household purchases have declined from about 70 percent of the GNP to about 60 percent. This is a real cost of the war industry in that the average household in the United States is only able to purchase about five-sixths of what it would be able to purchase in the absence of a war industry. In the world as a whole the world war industry must be regarded as a kind of potlatch,[2] a "waste grant" from the people of the world to nothing at all, which reduces not only present welfare but also future welfare below what it would otherwise be. The conclusion seems unavoidable—that the present international system is the most pathological of all segments of the world social system and that its control, modification, or even its abolition is one of the major items on the agenda of the human race.

The development of nuclear weapons has intensified the ultimately pathological nature of the international system, even though it may have given it a short-run stability. The nuclear weapon has accentuated the deterrence aspect of the system, as against conquest or tribute, and the system is sold to the public by its organizers as a system of stable deterrence. In the long run, however, deterrence cannot be stable, or it would cease to deter. If the probability of nuclear weapons going off were zero, this would be the same as not having them at all. Deterrence, therefore, most involve a positive probability, no matter how low, of deterrence breaking down and the actual carrying out of the threats of destruction. If there is positive probability of nuclear warfare, it is clear that if we wait long enough, it will happen. Even if the probability is only 1 percent per annum, this cumulates very uncomfortably in a hundred years.[3] Added to the $400 billion actual direct current cost of the world war industry, we have to add the discounted value of expected nuclear destruction, which is not an inconsiderable figure.

COMMENSALITY AND EXPANSIONISM

Because of the failure of the international system to deal with the problem of the world war industry, it still dominates the public grants economy. Nevertheless, there has been a small, quite perceptible shift, especially in the last generation, toward integrative grants rather than threat grants, as reflected especially in the long, slow, and fluctuating rise of what might be called genuine foreign aid. This phenomenon is all the more striking because in many ways it goes counter to the dynamics of the international threat system. A country's relative position in the threat system depends substantially on its level of economic development, especially as measured by its overall GNP. Consequently, if the international system were governed wholly by considerations of threat, one would not expect any nation to decrease its relative power by trying to increase the GNP of any other. It is an important indication, therefore, of the slow rise of the world integrative system that it is now almost universally recognized that richer nations have some sort of obligation to assist poorer nations in getting richer. Integrative foreign aid consists of grants made specifically with this end in view. The total volume of integrative foreign aid is still very small, certainly far below 1 percent of the GNP of the rich countries. It is hard to tell how much it is because of the mixture of integrative and threat grants, which almost all foreign aid programs involve. Nevertheless, the fact that it exists at all is significant. It represents an extension of the principle of commensality to all mankind. A family who sits around a table (*mensa* in Latin) is an example of an integrative grants economy. Food is distributed according to need, not according to any principle of exchange. Historically, the "table" has constantly been enlarging, from the family, to the clan, to the nation, and now to the whole earth. The analogy must not be pushed too far, however, for there are no parents presiding over the table at which the human race sits. It is a very large table, so that people on the other side of it may be quite invisible over the rim of the horizon. Nevertheless, it is this consciousness of the unity of mankind, however dim, that is behind the rise of foreign aid, and without it the international system would be left in a state of pure threat and counterthreat.

Mixed in with commensality is another principle that still has elements of the integrative or "love" side of the spectrum but is mixed with threat and fear. This principle might be called expansionism, and it has been a crucial element in the international system. It is desire on the part of a particular community to have more people associated with it and, hence, in some sense a larger identity for its individual members. Missionary religions are a good case in point, as a religious community devotes resources to the expansion of its particular faith. Almost all religions have alternating periods of expansionism and consolidation. Religions that claim universal validity—such as Christianity, Islam, and Buddhism—are particularly likely to be expansionist. Religions that are tied to local scenes and local gods—such as Shinto, Hinduism, or precaptivity Judaism—are much less likely to be expansionist.

In nations expansionism becomes imperialism, which again can take many forms, from crude conquests and exploitation of subject peoples, on the one hand, to more or less voluntary associations of nations, like the British Commonwealth, the French Community, or the Organization of American States, on the other. Religious and political expansionism often go together, as in the United Kingdom, France, and the United States in the nineteenth and early twentieth centuries, where the missionary enterprises of the churches and the political enterprises of the expanding empires frequently went hand in hand. It was often the same Britishers who sang, "Jesus shall reign where'er the sun/Doth his successive journies run" in church and then listened with approval to Elgar's *Land of Hope and Glory*, with its incredible verse: "Wider still and wider may thy bounds be set/God who made thee mighty, make thee mightier yet." Just as the missionary enterprises of British and American Protestantism were related to the expansion of the polity in which they lived, so the French Catholic missionary enterprise and the Russian Orthodox missionary enterprise had something to do with the development of the French Empire and the Russian Empire. Germany and Italy were latecomers to the expansionist field; Sweden abandoned expansionism in the seventeenth century after a considerable period of it; Portugal until 1974 was an interesting example of a fossilized expansionist society, putting a disproportionate amount of energy into resisting a contraction of its empire, the loss of which would certainly be beneficial to its own people. It, too, has now joined the crowd and liquidated its empire.

When one looks at the patterns of foreign aid, one sees very clearly that they are related to past expansionism, if not to present. The French put a relatively large proportion of their GNP into foreign aid, and they devote it almost entirely to the area of the old French Empire. The aid can almost be regarded as an expression of gratitude on the part of France to people who have the grace to speak French and have a French tradition, imposed on them in the old days by imperial France. It is, of course, always hard to disentangle the national security or the threat system aspects from the integrative aspects in foreign aid, but it is hard to believe that the French get much national security out of the aid that they give to Gabon or lose much out of the fact that they do not give much to "ungrateful" Guinea. Similarly, the British give a disproportionate amount of aid to the Commonwealth, and the United States has had an Alliance for Progress in Latin America. In the cases of the United States, the Soviet Union, and China there seems to be a larger strategic element in foreign aid, for these countries tend to support countries ideologically sympathetic to them. Ideology, however, seems to be quite a weak integrative system in comparison with nationalism and nationalist expansions, like the French Community and the British Commonwealth. Between the Soviet Union and East Germany the ideological community seemed to work in reverse, for up until 1956, at any rate, the East Germans were forced to make enormous grants to the Soviets, amounting in all perhaps to $12 billion,[4] and it is quite possible on balance that all the East European countries make net grants to the Soviet Union rather than receive grants from it. Soviet aid to the Chinese, likewise, even in the years before their split, was very small, amounting at most to a few cents per Chinese per annum. By contrast the internal grants economy within the Soviet Union seems to be quite substantial, although it is hard to get any figures for this. There seems little doubt, however, that the Russians have made substantial internal grants from the Russian Soviet Socialist Republic to the Uzbeks, Kazaks, and other non-Russian peoples within the Soviet Union, indicating again that national expansion is a much more powerful source of integrative relationship than ideological expansion and reflecting the fact, again, that the national community is the most powerful integrative system in the modern world. The People's Republic of China has likewise made large grants to Tibet and other parts of its non-Chinese "empire."

The purest integrative grants are those made by the smaller rich countries, such as the Scandinavian countries, where the political justification of foreign aid is quite deliberately an appeal to human community and sympathy, where no pretense is made that the grants are, in fact, exchanges from which the granting nation will receive some sort of subtle benefits, which is too frequently the argument used in the United States. The appeal here is really to benevolent national identity, and there is undoubtedly a demand, and perhaps a very large latent demand, for an appeal of this kind, especially for those who are already rich and reasonably secure.

When we look at the total determinants, therefore, of the propensity to make international grants, we shall not be surprised that this also presents an extremely complex and confused picture. We have, on the one hand, the spectrum of motivation from threat grants to integrative grants, which we have already noted. On the other hand, we have a problem of the perception of the efficiency of grants, and it is to this aspect of the problem that we must now turn.

EFFICIENCY OF GRANTS: EMERGENCY GRANTS

The *efficiency of grants* refers to the perception, especially on the part of the grantor, of what might be called the cost-effectiveness ratio—that is, the cost to him, on the one hand, and his perception of the value of the effect of the grant on the other. For example, in threat grants we see this in terms of the cost effectiveness of weapons: more bang (or deaths) for the buck. In integrative grants we see it in the cost effectiveness of transfers from the perspective of the welfare of the recipient. Here again, we have a spectrum ranging from what might be called emergency and relief grants on one side to long-run developmental grants on the other. Grants to victims of emergencies and disasters have long been a feature of social life, perhaps because disaster arouses pity and a sense of human community. We visualize ourselves in the position of the victims and are horrified at their distress. There may also be an element of fear insurance in this; we feel we might ourselves be in the same position some day, and it serves as a kind of informal insurance for all of us against misfortunes of this kind. Further-more, grants to people in temporarily desperate situations are clearly likely to have a high cost-effectiveness ratio. The dollar we give up from our own consumption, which may make a small difference to us, is the difference between life and death to the recipient. We will need to have only a small rate of benevolence to find it worthwhile to make the small sacrifices involved on the part of the donors. If I perceive that a sacrifice of $1 on my part is going to be worth at least $100 to the recipient, obviously I am getting the satisfactions of generosity very cheaply.

The great problem of emergency grants is that their magnitude depends on the visibility and the dramatic qualities of the emergency situation. Thus, the disaster in the Welsh mining village of Aberfan in 1966, when the mine dump collapsed and fell on the school, produced an extraordinary wave of compassion and a flow of contributions—about $10,000 per family—that was almost embarrassingly large to this small community. The much larger disaster of, say, East Pakistan (Bangladesh) in the floods of 1971 and the war of 1972 provoked a relatively smaller response—about $15 per head—perhaps because it was too large to be imagined, or perhaps also because the potential donors felt that anything they could give would be such a drop in the bucket that it would really make no difference to the colossal nature of the tragedy. There is, therefore, an almost built-in quality in the system that leads to the misallocation of emergency grants for relief in the private grants sector. While the public grants sector may counteract these disproportions somewhat, the public grants sector likewise is affected by the same kind of motivations that operate in the private grants sector. Governmental and intergovernmental relief is also likely to go to the more dramatic and more visible cases and to be concentrated on problems of moderate size. At both the private and the public level, when disasters are too small to be noticed, as well as when they are too large to be grasped, they will not arouse much public compassion.

A good example of a successful granting operation with a consider-able element of emergency grants was the Marshall Plan after World War II. Even though this plan was undoubtedly linked to strategic and threat system considerations, it also had a powerful element of emergency relief to fellow human beings. A good deal of political support for the Marshall Plan in the United States came from those who were emotionally affected by the postwar conditions in Europe and wanted to do something about it. In this case the effectiveness per dollar granted was very high, both in Western Europe and in the parallel operations in Japan. This type of postwar emergency grant had become a highly acceptable part of the international system, though the United States war with Vietnam was an exception. This rehabilitation even of former enemies—and more surprising, of potential enemies—is a very striking feature of the twentieth century and it is relatively new. It respresents the expansion of the very old human emotions of pity and sympathy into a much wider field.

DEVELOPMENT GRANTS

As we move from relief to reconstruction and from emergency grants to development grants, the picture becomes less clear and also less happy. Relief is fairly easy to do, and we usually know when we have done it. We give starving people food and they are no longer starving, at least for the moment. Development is not easy to do, and we often do not know when we have done it. Development grants, therefore, suffer from a very real problem of cost effectiveness, and where the grantor becomes uncertain about the effectiveness, he becomes much more sensitive to the cost.

Development can be defined as any change in the total state or condition of a society that increases its productivity in terms of human welfare. The fundamental input here is 24 hours a day of human living; the output is well-being, however inaccurately this can be measured. What we are really trying to measure is per capita welfare. A very crude and inaccurate measure is real national income per head, or real net national product per head. Even per capita welfare, however, is not the only significant variable. We have also seen that we cannot neglect the distributional aspects of this process and that if an increased per capita net national product, for instance, is all concentrated in 10 percent of the population, while 90 percent do not increase their welfare—even worse if they diminish it—then this condition cannot be regarded as development. Along with the average measure of per capita net national product, we must also include a measure of movement toward a more satisfactory distribution of income. An overall measure of development would be some kind of weighted average of these two, but what weight we would put on them depends, of course, on our internal value system. The radical egalitarian societies of Cuba and Maoist China put so high a weight on movement toward equality that they seem to have been willing to buy this with restricted development and political tyranny. At the other extreme we have societies that seem to put a zero weight on the distributional factor and are willing to move to much more unequal incomes if only that will increase the per capita net national product. These weights have to be evaluated, both by individuals and, through the political processes, by whole societies. There is no objective standard that can be applied, at least over a very wide range. The problem is made more complicated by the fact that there is no satisfactory single scalar index of distribution, for many different statistical moments of the distribution may be significant in its evaluation.[5]

However difficult development is to define or to measure, there is very wide agreement that the developmental process can be recognized and that it consists in an increase of knowledge, skill, and capital, which in turn amounts to an increase in the complexity of the structures in the society. We move, for instance, from short-handled hoes to long-handled hoes, to ox-driven plows, to tractors, perhaps ultimately to hydroponic production of articifial algae in greenhouses. In this process the cumulation of physical, nonhuman capital plays a significant role, but far more important is the cumulation of capital within the human nervous system— that is, the learning process. Development is a learning process and very little else. It does not consist merely of the piling up of all kinds of goods, capital accumulation in the simplest sense. It consists of developing stocks of new kinds of goods, and more important, it consists of developing skills and knowledge in the human nervous system that did not exist there before. It is by no means absurd to regard the whole capital accumulation process as essentially a learning process, not only in the sense that human learning is crucial to it but also in the sense that even physical capital really consists of human knowledge imposed on the physical world. The dictaphone and the typewriter by which this book is being produced originated in some corresponding structure in somebody's nervous system, which was then translated into the organized physical complexity of the dictaphone and the typewriter. Such objects certainly never exist in the absence of human knowledge.

However, if development is to take place, resources must be devoted to it. We must distinguish in all societies between what might be called the maintenance sector and the development sector. The maintenance sector replaces existing consumption with the production of people, objects, and knowledge of the same kind that is being consumed. The apple that is eaten is replaced by an apple that is grown. The house that is burned down is replaced by another house of exactly the same kind. Old people as they age, deteriorate, and die are replaced by a younger people with approximately the same kind of knowledge and ideas. This is the "open-system" aspect of society in that its structure is maintained in the midst of a throughput of people, materials, and information. If all the resources of a society are devoted to maintenance, obviously there will be no development, and society will simply reproduce itself generation after generation. There have been many historical examples of such stagnant societies. If a society is to develop, a certain portion of its activity must be devoted to development; the larger this proportion and the more efficiently it is used, the greater will be the rate of development.

AID VERSUS INVESTMENT

We can now begin to see the significance of the grants economy in the development process. A poor and unproductive society with little human knowledge and a primitive capital structure will have to spend almost all its resources on maintenance. Indeed, there is a strong tendency for societies in a given state of culture and technology to develop to the point that the entire resources of the society have to be devoted to maintaining the existing conditions. This is similar to the stationary state made familiar by the classical economists, and it is a condition that many societies, especially primitive societies, have approximated for long periods of time. Even complex and developed societies, like that of Mohenjo Daro, the ancient civilization of the Indus, seemed to maintain a steady state (if we can judge by the artifacts) for many hundreds of years. Classical China is an example of a society that reached a steady state at a fairly high level of development for the technology of its day. There is a tendency, therefore, for any developmental process to come to an end in a condition in which all resources are devoted to maintenance.

If society is to break out of this condition and start off on a new developmental process, there seem to be only two procedures it can use, although in different combinations. It may be able to release internal resources by some kind of reorganization or change in its patterns of life in such a way as to increase its total output beyond the maintenance level. It can do this by transferring people who are idle in agriculture, for instance, into industry or by operating its existing capital more intensively—for instance, by running factories on a three-shift basis rather than running them only eight hours a day. The other process consists of obtaining sources from outside, which it can then either devote directly to development or use to release resources from maintenance internally, which it can also devote to development. The net import of resources implies a short-run grant from the outside world in real terms. That is, for a stationary society to enter into this path of development it must be able to import more than it exports. This can be done either by deferred exchange or by grants. Deferred exchange is traditional foreign investment, either through contractual loans or an import surplus of goods to which foreigners retain title and from which they expect to derive profit in the future. From the developing country's point of view foreign investment is justified if the increase in productivity and the resulting growth in domestic income are larger than the interest and profit payments that have to be paid for it. Thus, to take a very simple example, suppose a country borrows $1 million and promises to repay $2 million in ten years. If with the real import surplus (excess of imports over exports) it obtains with the $1 million it is able to devote resources to capital construction or to education, which then increases the productivity of the people so that in ten years the national income has risen by more than the $1 million paid in interest, the excess is sheer gain, and the investment has been worth it to the developing country. If, however, the investment is devoted to unwise and unproductive purposes, the $1 million in interest is a burden on the future generations, imposed by the earlier generation; it is essentially an inter-generational transfer.

There are many examples of countries whose development has been materially assisted by foreign investment. On the other hand, there are also many examples in which foreign investment has not set off a sustained developmental process in the developing country and in which its costs, therefore, have been greater than the benefits. There are also cases in which the refusal to accept foreign investment (Burma may be a case in point) has prevented development. Obviously, the lower the rate of interest or profit a country has to pay, the better the chance that the investment will be advantageous for it. In the case of foreign aid that is an outright grant, the rate of interest, of course, is really minus infinity. If the rate of interest were zero, a country would pay back exactly the amount that it had borrowed. Obviously the chances of a direct grant being beneficial are much greater than that of any investment at a positive or even a finite negative rate of interest. Nevertheless, to rely on grants as a means of development is clearly to rely on a very small part of the total spectrum of short-run transfers, so that too much reliance on grants may severely limit the rate of development. We see this also in the case of individuals. Many more people have become rich by borrowing than have become rich by begging.

This does not mean that foreign aid is undesirable. We will be deluded, however, if we think that grants of this kind are likely to be a major factor in world development, at least in the present state of world community. The development of a small international grants economy is a very poor substitute, indeed, for a large system of efficient and well-safeguarded foreign investment, and grants, indeed, may be better used in the subsidization of foreign investment rather than in direct grants themselves. As the old Chinese proverb says, "It is better to give a poor man a fishing net than to give him fish." This is only true if he is a good fisherman. The proper balance between grants and investments is still a problem that requires a great deal more work.

NOTES

1. An arms race is a process by which at a given level of armaments in one nation, A, another nation, B, increases its armaments, which induces A to increase its armaments, which

induces *B* to increase its armaments still further, and so on, until either some equilibrium is reached or the system explodes into war.

2. A potlatch was a ceremony among the Indians of the northwest coast of North America in which individuals gained prestige by the destruction of large quantities of blankets and other useful goods.

3. The probability of an event of a 1 percent per annum probability (like a hundred years' flood) happening at some unknown date within a hundred years is about 63 percent; within 400 years it is 98.4 percent.

4. Heinz Kohler, *Economic Integration in the Soviet Bloc* (New York: Praeger, 1966).

5. Suppose that the bottom *x* percent of the population received *y* percent of the total income. If incomes were perfectly equal, then $x = y$ for all values of *x*. Any 10 percent of the population will get 10 percent of the income; any 20 percent will get 20 percent, and so on. One measure of inequality is the Gini index, which is $\Sigma\ y/x$. Thus a society in which the bottom 10 percent of the population gets 2 percent of the total income is presumably more equal than one in which the bottom 10 percent gets only 1 percent of the total income. Suppose, however, that the poor get richer and both the middle class and the rich get poorer, in contrast to the situation in which the poor get richer, the rich get poorer, and the middle class remains the same. These two situations might easily have the same Gini index but very different kinds of redistributions.

7

The Welfare Economics of Grants

THE GOODNESS FUNCTION

Economics has never been content to be positive—that is, merely descriptive of fact and indifferent to values. It has always had a strong normative and evaluative streak, even from the days of Adam Smith. It has, however, been concerned with separating the positive facts from the normative values and has also insisted that any normative economics be based firmly on some kind of positive knowledge of the nature and dynamics of the system itself. Things do not exist merely because they are right and good, and a thing cannot be right and good if it cannot exist. There is no point in evaluating completely imaginary and nonexistent systems. Nevertheless, the urge to evaluate has been strong, and much of the motivation for the study of economics has come out of it. Positive economics is mainly a kind of celestial mechanics of the prices and quantities of commodities. Normative economics is an attempt to do orderly evaluations of these dynamic processes and to suggest which are better and which are worse. Critics may point out the parallel that "normative astronomy" is astrology. The fallacy of astrology, however, is not that we should not be interested in whether the planets affect the condition of humans but just that there is very little real evidence that they do. The terrestial mechanics of the prices and quantities of commodities clearly does affect the condition of humans. Hence, normative economics is a legitimate intellectual discipline, for it is sensible to ask whether condition A of the economy—or in more broad terms, the social system—is better or worse than condition B.

The most general concept of normative social science is what economists have called, perhaps rather unfortunately, a welfare function, better, perhaps, called a "goodness function," which can be written as equation 7.1:

$$W = F \text{ (the relevant universe).} \tag{7.1}$$

W is simply a number, which we can call goodness. It does not usually even have to be cardinal (1, 2, 3 . . .), for ordinal numbers (first, second, third . . .) will often do just as well. Thus when W goes up, things are better; when it goes down, things are worse. I have simply called the argument of the function the relevant universe. It supposes that the state of the universe, or at least the part of it that is relevant to each particular case, can be mapped into some kind of welfare field. That is, corresponding to each state of the universe we can postulate some level of goodness. We do not even have to assume that W is a single monotonic variable. We could write the equation as equation 7.2:

$$(W_1, W_2, W_3, \ldots W_n) = F \text{ (the relevant universe).} \tag{7.2}$$

In this equation W_1 measures whether person (or group) 1 feels better or worse off, W_2 does the same for person 2, and so on to W_n, so that any state of the universe can be mapped into a welfare space for as many parties or groups of parties as we wish. When we do this, of course, we cannot get any unequivocal answers to the question of whether state of the universe A is better or worse than state B. There may, indeed, be no such answer, even though we always have a strong tendency to look for it in the form of a function like equation 7.1. We may not be able to get much further, however, than the form of equation 7.2.

The argument of the function, what I have called the relevant universe, is going to consist of a large number of indexes, indicators, variables of all kinds, some of which can be represented by numbers, some by a range of positions, some perhaps just by presence or absence. The critical problem might almost be called the "which-way-is-up problem"; that is, if we have a variable in the relevant universe, call it A, the critical question is the sign of the differential dW/dA, that is, the increase in W divided by the increase in A. If A goes up, does W go up or does it go down? Those variables in which the sign of the differential is positive— that is, the more the better—can be called goods; those in which the sign is negative—the more the worse—can be called bads. There is not always agreement about which variables are goods and which are bads, although there are wide areas in which agreement is substantial. Almost everyone agrees that health is a good and sickness is a bad or that pleasure is a good and pain is a bad.

We run into trouble because some of these relationships, perhaps most of them, are nonlinear—that is, dW/dA is not constant. Some things are good when there is a little of them and become bad when there is a lot of them. This is the principle of the Aristotelian mean. Even quite simple variables exhibit this property. Thus, if we are evaluating body temperature, we find that somewhere between 98° and 99° Farenheit is best and that temperatures either higher than this or lower than this are worse than the ideal body temperature. One suspects that nearly all the variables of the welfare function eventually exhibit this kind of nonlinearity. The prolongation of life of a young person is clearly a good; for an incapacitated and senile nonagenarian prolongation of life may clearly be a bad. There is an ideal age of death, just as there is an ideal body temperature. The only reason we fail to recognize this is that up to the present century by far the largest number of people died before the optimum age, so that an increase in the life-span has always seemed to be good. Now, however, we are beginning to realize that life is also a nonlinear function; beyond a certain point increase in the life-span is a bad.

Generally speaking, the more complex the variable, the more heterogeneous the realities to which it refers and the harder it is to find agreement on the position of the optimum. Thus, if we try to answer the question, Is more socialism good or bad? we will run into difficulties of what kind of socialism. Socialism is a complex collection of variables and cannot be measured on a single numerical scale like a ruler. We may also find ourselves in considerable disagreement about where the optimum point of the function is. The same would be true of any complicated social variables, such as freedom or justice, or even wealth. An increase in wealth is almost universally agreed to be good for poor people; it is by no means obvious that it is good for rich people. But again it is very hard to say where the optimum point lies.

Another significant aspect of the which-way-is-up problem arises because of the complex interrelationships of the variables within the argument of the welfare function. It is very rare, indeed, to be able to change one variable of the complex universe without at the same time changing others. An economist would say that all things are joint products. That is, if we increase A, we are going to find that we may increase B, we may decrease C, and so on, all across the board. Consequently, when we ask ourselves the question, Is an increase in A good or bad? we also have to take into consideration that increasing A is going to increase B, decrease C, and so on, and the effects of these are going to have to be evaluated. In recent years we have become particularly aware of the fact that these joint products include both goods and bads and that it is often very hard to increase a good without at the same time increasing a bad. This is the essence of the environmental problem as it relates to pollution and exhaustion. We have pollution, which is the increase in something that we widely regard as bad, not because there are wicked people who like to pollute things but because an increase in A, which is good, also produces an increase in B, which is bad, and may lead to a diminution in C, which is also a good. Thus, the production of electric power, which is clearly a good, also produces an increase in smoke and atmospheric pollution, which is bad. It also results in a diminution of the reserves of fossil fuels, which is the diminution of a good, so that in making a total evaluation, we have to take into account the effects of all these changes on W. It is not only difficult to get to know what the real internal production functions are, so that we know what bads are produced with what goods, but it is also frequently difficult to evaluate these things in terms of goodness.

The famous old economic principle of diminishing marginal utility can be brought in to illustrate some of these problems. This is logically very much the same principle as the Aristotelian mean in that it postulates a relationship between any variable of the universe and the goodness index W of the form of Figure 7.1, where we measure variable A horizontally and welfare vertically. The "marginal goodness," a concept that corresponds to marginal utility, is the slope or gradient of this curve at any point; it is the amount that W increases for a unit increase of A. It is positive to the left of N, negative to the right of N, and zero at N, where the goodness index W reaches a maximum. Anywhere to the left of M, A is a

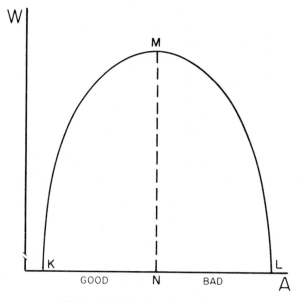

Figure 7.1 The Goodness Function

good and an increase of A increases goodness. Anywhere to the right of M, however, A is a bad and an increase in A diminishes goodness. The position of the point M, of course, differs sharply with different variables, but the general form of the relationship is extremely common. One very important conclusion of this analysis is that things are more likely to be good when we have a little of them and to be bad when we have a lot of them. This is why, for instance, poor countries and poor people are willing to put up with a lot of pollution. As they used to say in Lancashire, "Where there's muck, there's munny." If there is not very much munny—that is, real goods—an increase in goods will be valued very highly; and an increase in the bads that go along with it may not be valued highly enough to counteract the value of the increased goods.

Any general description of a function that includes the whole universe in its argument, is, of course, absurd. Nevertheless, there have been attempts to delineate certain segments or portions of the goodness function, which may turn out to be very useful. We must emphasize that the goodness function is not a vague abstraction. This is something we encounter almost every moment of our lives—every decision, every act is based on some sort of evaluation of its consequences, according to our private goodness function. Even though the so-called theory of maximizing behavior, of which economists are very fond, may say formally little more than, "Everybody does what is thought best at the time," it does at least point up the principle that all behavior involves evaluation of alternative futures. If some kind of descriptive content can be put into the evaluation or goodness function, the analysis can take on a good deal of content and may even be helpful in clarifying actual decisions.

BENEVOLENCE AND THE PARETIAN OPTIMUM

The body of thought known as welfare economics was a courageous attempt to try to put content into the general welfare or goodness function, particularly in the critical form of equation 7.1, where we try to answer the question, Is state A of the universe better or worse than state B for the human race as a whole? Even in the formal sense, the attempt failed.

Paul Samuelson demonstrated we could never be absolutely sure that one commodity mix was better than another. Kenneth Arrow demonstrated that there was no general, mechanical way of summing individual preferences into a group or social preference function. This left the formal structure pretty much in ruins.[1] Nevertheless, the effort was well worthwhile and should by no means be written off. It was an attempt to answer the question, What do we really mean when we say that one state of the system is better or worse than another, speaking professionally as economists?

The crucial concept of welfare economics is that of the Paretian optimum, named for the Italian economist Vilfredo Pareto. This is perhaps most easily stated in a negative form—that the system is *not* in the Paretian optimum if by any rearrangements at least one person can be made better off in his own estimation and no other person is worse off in his own estimation. This avoids the difficult problem of comparability of the welfare of different persons, and while it produces a large optimum set of social variables rather than a single point, it at least points the way to a rather careful definition of *positive-sum games*, or processes in society that make everybody better off, or at least no worse off. We need not here specify the actual conditions for a Paretian optimum. The reader can find these in the literature.[2] Perhaps the principal value of the Paretian optimum is that it does point toward identifying conditions and processes of society that are clearly pathological. If, for instance, there is some arrangement of the social system that is theoretically obtainable and that would make some people better off and nobody worse off, then the system is not a Paretian optimum. If the dynamics of the system clearly prevent any movement toward the Paretian optimum and, indeed, create a movement away from it, this is almost overwhelming evidence that this particular dynamic is pathological. We see this, for instance, in such things as the "prisoner's dilemma" game,[3] in which the dynamics of the situation, as for instance in an arms race or a quarrel, push both parties from positions where both of them are better off to positions where both of them are worse off. In many social situations it is quite easy to postulate another condition in the system in which almost everybody is better off than they are now; if the dynamics of the system move in the opposite direction, it is surely pathological almost beyond doubt.

For all the usefulness of the concept the formal analysis of the Paretian optimum has some severe defects. It assumes in the first place that the preferences of individuals are given, cannot be further inquired into, and are not subject to change. From any view of social dynamics this is almost hopelessly unrealistic. The truth is that preferences are learned in the course of the socialization of the individual. We adjust our preferences to our opportunities, just as much as we seek to adjust our opportunities to our preferences. This is what I have sometimes called the "sour grapes" principle—if we find that we cannot get something, we decide that we do not want it. The whole Buddhist, indeed much Eastern, philosophy is based on the principle that the way to get what you want is not to want much. Even at more mundane levels, the whole apparatus of what might be called the persuasion industry—advertising, selling, preaching, propaganda, education, arguments, and so on—is all directed toward changing people's preferences; thus, it seems particularly unfortunate to develop a theory based on the assumption that preferences do not change. On the other hand, we also have to admit that if we are to evaluate changes in preferences, we must have some system of superpreferences by which to evaluate the change, so we may perhaps get back to Pareto at one remove. We do, indeed, regard some forms of persuasion as more legitimate than others. We also often find strong convictions that some preferences, even our own, are unwise. The whole distinction in practical moral philosophy between the passions and the will suggest at least that there are two levels, and perhaps more, at which evaluations can be made—that is, a set of preferences that constitutes the passions can be criticized by a superior set that constitutes the will.

Another weakness of Paretian welfare economics is that it tends to assume *selfishness*—that is, independence of individual welfare functions—which supposes that the welfare of one person is not affected by his perceptions of the welfare of others. This is a preposterous limitation. I argue that selfishness is merely the zero point on a scale of benevolence and malevolence and, hence, is likely to be very rare. Benevolence may be measured by the rate of benevolence, the rate of benevolence of A toward B being how much A will sacrifice in order to perceive that B is better off by some unit amount. If we think in terms of a monetary measure, if A will give up 20 cents in order to perceive that B is better of by a dollar, his rate of benevolence toward B is 0.2. A negative rate of benevolence is a rate of malevolence. If the rate of benevolence of A toward B is -0.2, this means that A would be willing to give up 20 cents in order to perceive that B was worse off by a dollar. If it cost the United States \$4 to do \$1 worth of damage in North Vietnam, the rate of benevolence of the United States toward North Vietnam was about -4. Selfishness, of course, would be simply a zero rate of benevolence. That is, A would not be willing to sacrifice anything in order to perceive that B is either better or worse off by a dollar. Selfishness in this sense is likely only between people who are quite ignorant of each other and have no relationships. The moment people enter into relationships they tend to develop either benevolence or malevolence to some degree.

It is not too difficult to develop a concept of an extended Paretian optimum to take account of benevolence and malevolence. Whereas the Paretian optimum in the narrow sense confines itself entirely to the exchange economy, the extended Paretian optimum clearly has to include grants. The formal condition for the extended optimum is that each two-party relationship should proceed to the point that any further extension of the relationship or the transfers would be regarded by at least one party as bringing in only as much additional utility as he paid out in utility. Theoretically, this would give some sort of optimum, or at least an optimum set, of grants matrices—the grants matrix being a matrix showing the total grants between any two pairs of people, just as the traditional Paretian optimum gives an optimum set of exchange matrices.

THREAT IN THE PARETIAN OPTIMUM

If benevolence-induced gifts were the only form of grants, we could perhaps leave the matter at the present point of analysis. Unfortunately, however, as we have seen, grants proceed out of threat as well as out of benevolence. The problem of expanding the Paretian optimum type of concept to include tribute is by no means easy. As we have seen, we cannot dismiss the threat system as totally pathological, for there are legitimate threats involved, for instance, in the tax system, or in the legal system generally, which almost certainly increase general welfare. One has a strong intuition, however, that the threat system is highly subject to pathological dynamic processes and that any simple extension of the Paretian principles to include the threat system is precluded by the fact we have noted before: that in the algebra of social systems two negatives are not the same thing as a positive and that the abstention from producing a bad cannot be regarded as equivalent to producing a good. Thus, suppose we go back to the two-party relationship, and suppose that A by producing a threat to B induces B to make him a grant of a commodity. The formal conditions for the extended Paretian optimum may be fulfilled when, for instance, B extends the grant to the point that further extension would be regarded as not worth the value of the chance of loss, if A carries out the threat. B here is weighing a certain cost of submission to the threat as against the uncertain cost of defiance. This, however, simply assumes the existence of the threat and neglects the fact that making the threat in the first place has social cost, that is, creates negative capital.

This situation, incidentally, illustrates another weakness of the classical Paretian optimum—it assumes that all utility or welfare functions are continuous and takes no account of discontinuities and step functions. In the case of threat defiance may be all or none, although it may be defiance in response to a demand to increase the tribute marginally. A marginal increase in tribute, however, may have to be balanced against the chance of nonmarginal consequences of defiance. If B refuses the extra dollar, A may come down on him with the full capability of his threat. There seems to be no way of making social evaluation of the threat without interpersonal comparisons of utility, which welfare economics generally tries to avoid. If, however, we are to develop a general goodness function, there is really no way in which these interpersonal comparisons and personal evaluations can be avoided. Thus, in the above example in which we suppose B is making a transfer to A under conditions of threat, if the social welfare function of A is very highly valued so that an increase in his welfare has a high weight, whereas B is regarded as a no-good and a worthless fellow whose disutilities do not matter very much, then our social evaluation will prefer the condition in which B loses something that does not matter much and A gains something that does. Social apologetics for exploitation, imperialism, slavery, conscription, and other forms of threat-induced transfer usually go along these lines.

The evaluative situation becomes even more difficult when we introduce counterthreat, that is, deterrence. In the above example, B may respond not only by submission or defiance, but he may respond by a counterthreat, saying to A in effect, "If you do something nasty to me, I will do something nasty to you, so I am not going to give you anything." His counterthreat may reestablish the status quo before the introduction of threat and is likely to diminish tribute. We recall the famous American legend of "Millions for defense, but not a penny for tribute." On the other hand, under many circumstances tribute is cheaper than defense; the cost to B of producing a credible counterthreat would be more than the tribute he has to pay to A in response to A's threat. Indeed, if this were not so, nobody would pay taxes and government would be impossible.

An additional complication is introduced into the system by the fact that it is the credibility of threats that is significant in affecting behavior, and this credibility frequently tends to depreciate if threats are not carried out. Credibility is only loosely related to capability in the first place, and capability itself is a function of two variables—the means and the will. A may be armed to the teeth but may not have the will to use the arms. Where threats are not exercised, even though the physical means of carrying out the threat remain, the will may erode and the threatened party may believe that the will has eroded even when it has not. Consequently, in any threat system there is a positive probability that the threat will be carried out. Both submission and deterrence may erode into defiance. In estimating the cost of the threat system, therefore, the probability of the actual carrying out of the threat must be taken into consideration. The whole history of international relations is testimony to this principle. War is always either a breakdown of a threat-submission system or the breakdown of a deterrence system. It is easy to prove that stable deterrence is impossible in the long run, for if deterrence were really stable, it would soon cease to deter. That is, if the probability of threats being carried out were zero, their credibility would soon disappear. If, however, there is a positive probability of threats being carried out, then over a long enough period they will be carried out. Thus, the costs of threats being carried out have to be reckoned as part of the cost of the total system. Even without committing ourselves to interpersonal comparisons of utility then, the negative-sum aspect of the threat system can be identified and at least conceptually measured, first, in terms of the cost of all goods foregone because of the resources devoted to achieving the means of threat and, second, the cost in terms of any particular behavior probability of the present value of the bads that would actually be produced if the threats were carried out.

When we introduce dynamic considerations into the goodness or valuation functions, the difficulties become compounded, and one almost despairs of finding even partial solutions to the problem. How, for instance, do we evaluate transfers between the generations or between the present generation and posterity? If the present generation makes sacrifices in order that its posterity may have an easier time, this is certainly part of the intertemporal grants economy. The famous question, "What has posterity ever done for me?" must be taken seriously. Making sacrifices for a distant posterity is clearly the purest form of grants economy that can be imagined, for there can be no vestige of exchange in it. The only conceivable answer to this question is that in order to establish a satisfactory identity one must maintain some sort of community, however uncertain and discounted, not only with one's own day but with the whole human race as it stretches out through time and space. Here one could perhaps appeal also to the principle of serial reciprocity. The present generation has received a large inheritance from its ancestors in capital, knowledge, artifacts, culture, organizations, and so on, which it could not possibly have created by itself. This gift creates a sense of obligation that can only be expressed by conserving and even increasing the heritage to be passed on to the next generation. This, again, however, supposes some kind of community extending over time.

TOPOLOGY OF THE GOODNESS FUNCTION

One thinks of the general goodness function as a great mountain that each person, and the human race as a whole, is trying to climb—the higher the better. In traditional economic theory the mountain is steep and is bathed in the pellucid sunshine of eighteenth century rationality. There are, of course, fences across it so that we cannot get to the top, the fence being what economists call the possibility boundary—that which divides the achievable from the nonachievable. However, we always know which way is up, and we go directly to the highest point the fence permits and presumably stay there rejoicing. This is the theory of maximizing behavior. It has always amused me that what the economist calls an equilibrium of behavior, psychologists tend to call frustration. Economic man, having perfect mental health, proceeds to his best obtainable position, then industriously starts digging around the fenceposts to move the fence that bounds him in. Psychological man, on reaching the fence, screams and agonizes because he cannot climb over it.

My own view of the goodness mountain, "the Hill of the Lord," as the Psalmist calls it (Psalm 24:3), is very different. I see large parts of it as a great rolling plateau, shrouded in mist, in which it is quite difficult to know whether one is going up or down, in which different places, although widely separated, may be at the same height of goodness. Under these circumstances the best may be the enemy of the good, and the legitimate search for the better degenerates to a neurotic inability to be content with anything, which easily leads to sliding downhill rather than climbing uphill. Furthermore, I visualize this plateau as having cliffs, places where movement in our social space leads to disaster and catastrophic declines in welfare, even perhaps to irretrievable disaster. One of the major tasks of evaluative analysis, therefore, is to identify these cliffs and to build artificial fences around them. The fences, of course, are the "no-no's," the prohibitions, both ethical and legal, that arise out of the past experience of observing people, or even whole societies, fall over cliffs. Unfortunately, falling over cliffs is a very bad method for learning about them. And as there is no very good alternative method for learning about cliffs, it is not surprising that our knowledge of where they lie is very inadequate. We build fences where there are no cliffs and we leave dangerous cliffs unfenced. Both of these conditions are dangerous. If we build fences where there are no cliffs, people will eventually jump over the fences, find no cliffs on the other side of them, and so decide there are no cliffs at all—and hence may trot along merrily through the mist and fall over the next cliff. What might be called sumptuary morality or legislation is full of examples of this kind. Another little drink will not do us any harm, until sometime it does. Freedom can lead to benefit or to disaster, depending on the circumstances. In this modest view of evaluative analysis, therefore, we abandon the futile search for the top of the goodness mountain, and we concentrate on trying to identify its cliffs—that is, its clearly pathological regions.

Let us return, then, to the system of one-way transfers or grants and ask ourselves whether we identify what we might modestly call probably pathological processes, or deteriorating systems, in which there will be wide agreement that the process goes from bad to worse rather than from bad to better. I have sometimes called these processes "traps," simply because the beginning of the process, like the piece of cheese in the mousetrap, often looks quite attractive; yet once we are embarked on the process, the trap closes and we find ourselves in a deteriorating system from which it is very hard to escape. In my book *The Meaning of the Twentieth Century*,[4] for instance, I identify three major traps of this kind, which I call the "population trap," "the war trap," and the "entropy trap." Unrestrained population growth can bring any development to frustration and can lead to the almost endless proliferation of human misery. The reliance on threat and counterthreat to achieve defense leads into disastrous proliferation in the production of bads. The unrestricted utilization of natural resources and geological capital may mean that development is simply speeding up the day when everything will be gone.

THE SACRIFICE TRAP

Just as the total system has its traps, so does the segment we are studying under the heading of the grants economy. The first I call the "sacrifice trap." A grant is a sacrifice we may make in the interests of our identity, for our identity depends very largely on the community with which we identify. If this community demands sacrifices from us, our identification with it is reinforced. It is very hard for people to admit that their previous sacrifices have been in vain and that the community on behalf of which they have been made is unworthy of them. We resist threats to our own identity. Consequently, it is easy to get locked into an identity that may demand too much sacrifice. Sacrifice creates sacredness. Sacredness, like every other virtue, as we have seen, becomes a vice if there is too much of it, following the famous principle of the Aristotelian mean. The dynamics of the sacrifice trap, however, suggest that we are constantly in danger of getting too much sacredness to the point that it is no longer a useful organizer of society and so becomes pathological. Thus, the blood of the martyrs is the seed of the church but does not guarantee the truth of its doctrines. The blood of its soldiers is the seed of the state but does not guarantee that it will be a good society. The agonies of the student are the seed of the alumni association but do not guarantee that the college will do a good job. The tears of the children are the seed of the family but do not necessarily produce a rich nurturing of mentally healthy people. Good money is often thrown after bad but does not necessarily redeem it. One gets a depressing feeling sometimes that the people who are most admired by the human race and who are regarded as its heroes are precisely those who have created the maximum amount of human misery. Those who have demanded sacrifice—the prophets and conquerors, the revolutionaries, and the visionaries—are those who created the great phyla of human history. Those who have made things a little better for little people—the traders, the producers, the inventors, even the bankers—have no monuments and receive no eulogies.

The defense of the human race against the sacrifice trap is an unsolved problem. Defense against one fanaticism often produces another; defense against one sacrifice-produced identity involves sacrifice and so produces another. However, we cannot solve the problem by denying all sacrifice and all sacredness, for up to a point both sacrifice and sacredness give meaning and significance to human life and are positive values. The real problem is how do we desacralize those institutions that become too sacred? In the case of the church we have seen a retreat from an excess of sacredness over considerable parts of the world. The sacredness of the church and religious institutions generally has declined to the point that it is rarely pathological. People nowadays rarely kill or die because of their identity as a Lutheran or as a Catholic. We find exceptions to this in Northern Ireland, which is in the grip of a highly pathological sacrifice trap in religion. We find it also in Vietnam and Kampuchea, which have been, and still are, in the throes of the political sacrifice trap, also with religious and ideological overtones. One of the great problems of the world today is the desacralization of the nation-state to the point that it would seem just as absurd to kill or die for one's country as it would be for General Motors or for Calvinistic Methodism.

THE DEPENDENCY TRAP

Another pathological process in the grants sector is the dependency trap in which grants designed to meet a temporary need create such a successful adaptation to them that the need becomes permanent, so that grants actually create the situation in which they are perceived as neces- sary. The famous example in classical economics is the infant industry argument for tariffs or other forms of government grants. Assistance is given to a particular industry that could not survive if it were small but if it is protected or subsidized can grow to the point that it is self-sufficient, allowing for the withdrawal of protection or subsidization. Unfortunately, these infants have a way of not growing up. Vested interests are created, the grants are capitalized, and it becomes extremely difficult to do away with them; thus, we get a chronic distortion of the economy, which in the long run could be very costly. In general we could say that subsidies for people to stay where they are are apt to be pathological, as opposed to subsidies for people to change. There may be an exception if the social costs of rapid change are too high, in which case grants to slow down change may also be desirable.

Many other examples of the dependency trap could be given. We see this sometimes at the psychological level in the family, where grants of all kinds from a parent to a child produce a dependency from which the child may never be able to escape. Indeed, adolescent revolt is an essential element in the escape from the dependency trap so easily engendered in the parent-child relationship. One also gets a reverse phenomenon—the dependency of the parents on the children for emotional support and for giving meaning and significance to life. Unless there is a "menopause revolt" of the parents against the children, they are apt to be faced with the empty nest problem, which is supposed to be one of the major traumas of late middle life, though I must confess that my own empty nest seems agreeably spacious.

We get a similar phenomenon in the colonial-imperial relationship. It is all too easy for colonies to become almost permanently dependent upon the mother country for organizational skills and leadership. The liquidation of the colonial empire in the last 25 years has many parallels to an adolescent revolt, but in many cases it has been more like the mother bird pushing the babies out of the next than the babies revolting. But this breakaway from dependency is often very costly and traumatic. For example, the enormous human suffering that followed the abandonment of British rule in Nigeria, Uganda, and the Indian subcontinent and, even more, the unspeakable tragedy of Kampuchea were high costs to pay for independence. Sometimes it seems that this cost has to be paid, although one should always be concerned with how to reduce it.

One finds the same phenomenon of the dependency trap in welfare programs, such as Aid to Dependent Children, which may easily produce a welfare subculture permanently dependent on welfare grants and incapable of making possible adaptations toward genuine independence. We see the same phenomenon in the United States in the Indian reservations, which are perhaps one of the most disastrous examples of an acute dependency trap. This phenomenon is so widespread and so important that it is surprising that it has received so little serious consideration in the hands of social scientists, who have perhaps fallen into the dependency trap themselves.

THE IGNORANCE TRAP

The third trap of the grants sector is the ignorance trap, which arises because of the absence of feedback and the extraordinary difficulty of developing information systems that can report the consequences of grants and so report any divergences between the objectives of grants and their actual consequences. We noticed this phenomenon earlier and called it the principle of implicit irony. There is very little organized research and information collection and processing on these problems of the distributional effects of different policies. This may arise out of a subconscious feeling that ignorance is bliss—that if people knew how they were being affected by various policies, whether defense, conservation, or even social welfare policies, conflicts would become apparent and society would fall apart under the sheer difficulty of conflict management. On the other side, it can be argued that it is precisely our ignorance about the distributional effects of policies that creates incoherent frustration and anxiety that is corrosive of political legitimacy and stability. The feeling that whatever we do has totally unexpected consequences is intensively corrosive of the whole political order and is a major source of that rising wave of anomie, violence, and anarchism that represents perhaps the greatest threat to complex organized societies. While ignorance may be bliss in the short run, it is rarely bliss in the long run. We are left with the problem of how to improve the information processes and the feedback processes from grants behavior of all kinds—from private charity to foundations to governments, all of which are constantly doing harm in the name of doing good. Good intentions are no excuse for bad results, and the arrogance of the ignorant good-doers turns them into do-gooders and undermines that necessary function of doing real good, without which society cannot exist for very long.

One is tempted to suggest that in addition to the now required Environmental Impact Statement every policy or program should have a "Distributional Impact Statement" stating who will be benefited and who will be injured by the proposal, that is , what would be the impact on the grants system, both explicit and implicit. The drafting of such statements, however, would present a challenge to economists, in the present state of the art, that they might not be able to meet.

NOTES

1. For an excellent introduction to welfare economics with a good selective bibliography and a British slant, see Katherine M. Price, *Welfare Economics in Theory and Practice* (New York and London: Macmillan, 1977).

2. The original development of Pareto's ideas is best found in his *Manual of Political Economy*. See Vilfredo Pareto, *Manual of Political Economy*, trans. Ann S. Schwier and Alfred N. Page (1909; New York: Macmillian, 1972). My own exposition can be found in K. E. Boulding, "Welfare Economics," in *A Survey of Contemporary Economics*, ed. B. Haley, vol. 2 (Homewood, Ill.: Richard D. Irwin, 1952).

3. Anatol Rapoport and A. Chammah, *Prisoner's Dilemma: A Study in Conflict and Cooperation* (Ann Arbor: University of Michigan Press, 1965).

4. K. E. Boulding, *The Meaning of the Twentieth Century* (New York: Harper & Row, 1964).

8

An Epilogue on Time's Arrow

TYPES OF PROJECTIONS OF THE FUTURE

Up to this point this book has dealt with fairly straightforward phenomena and reasonably answerable questions, although some of the questions, especially about distribution, are hard to answer and are not answered yet. It is hard to take leave of the subject, however, without a look at some of the larger and perhaps unanswerable questions relating to the future. What is the wave, or are the waves, of the future? Are we, for instance, moving toward a society in which grants will make an increasing part of the whole body of transactions, until exchange is reduced to something quite vestigial? Or are we likely to find this period of increasing grants coming to an end and reaching some sort of equilibrium, and if so, at what level? Are we moving toward a society in which public grants will make up an increasing part of the whole? Or are we moving toward a freer society in which most of what is necessary is done out of spontaneous goodwill? Do we look forward to increasing equality, or do we contemplate a world of increasing inequality and exploitation? Most of us will not live to answer these questions. Nevertheless, they haunt our imaginations, and perhaps the ghosts of the future can only be exorcised by poetic speculation in the present.

The only way in which we can have any knowledge about the future is to make some sort of projections from our image of the past on the assumption that the past and the future are part of a continuum. At least four kinds of processes can be distinguished in our image of the past that enable us to make some sort of projections. First are the simple mechanical processes by which we project either stability or recurrence—the house was here yesterday, it is here today, and it will be here tomorrow—or constant rates of change, as when we estimate the position of a moving car in the next five seconds, or a constant acceleration, or even higher orders. The astronomer's celestial mechanics are, of course, the great success in mechanical prediction. In social systems we are much less successful in mechanical prediction. Even population projections based on mechanical assumptions about cohort changes and specific birth and death rates have let us down very badly and, indeed, have almost universally been wrong. Projections for economic growth have also turned out to be very disappointing, even those that are quite sophisticated and involve large numbers of variables. The real difficulty here is that unless we can find constant parameters for these systems, projection is impossible. In social systems especially the parameters of our mechanical models are frequently subject to unexpected shifts.

A second form of projection is the genetic, in which we have a system with a blueprint, whether in the form of a gene or in the form of an architect's plan, or even a five-year plan for a corporation or a socialist country. If there is an apparatus for carrying out the plan, we have some confidence in projecting it into the future. Thus, at the biological level we have every expectation that a kitten, if it survives, will grow up into a cat and not into a dog. We expect a building to look like its blueprint, and we expect at least a certain percentage of freshmen to graduate in four years. Failures at projection here are due mainly to breakdowns in the apparatus for carrying out the plan, assuming that it is realistic in the first place, with death in the case of the animal, tornadoes in the case of the building, or wars and social breakdown in the carrying out of social plans.

The third process in which we observe patterns through time is evolution. This includes the dynamic interaction of different species leading to the decline of some and to the extinction or survival of others. It also includes mutation, which changes the equations of dynamic interaction of the species. These patterns can be perceived in the long course of evolutionary history, beginning even with the evolution of the elements and going on to biological and social evolution. They can also be perceived in the human learning process, which has many parallels with evolution. The model has very little predictive power simply because almost the only way to detect evolutionary potential is after the fact—that is, after the potential has been realized. In our part of the universe evolution seems to have proceeded from the simple to the complex and, in this sense, has a "time's arrow" built into it. I know of no demonstration, however, that this must be so; and there are many places, such as the moon, where evolution stopped 3.5 billion years ago and never seems to have gotten much beyond the level of complexity of inorganic chemistry. There are clearly no principles in nature that say that evolutionary movement toward complexity has to continue beyond any given point;

thus, it would be risky to deduce that since both biological and social evolution has proceeded along these lines in the past, it will continue to do so in the future. There is very little evidence of reversal of evolutionary process in the earth's history, although, again, there is no reason to suppose that it would be impossible to have it reversed by some catastrophe.

The fourth pattern of time process might be called processes of constraint in which something about the environment of the system constrains its development beyond a certain point. An example is pouring tea into a teacup—a fairly simple mechanical system with the amount of tea in the cup growing at the rate in which it is coming in from the teapot. We know that if this continues very long, the teacup will overflow, and the size of the teacup is a constraint on the future of the process. The growth of animals from the fertilized egg into adulthood is a bit like the teacup. The growth process goes on until it is constrained by the inability of systems to grow without changing their proportions. Similarly, populations of any particular species will expand into a niche; they may expand rapidly at first, but as the niche begins to fill up, the rate of growth will eventually decline to zero.

Of these four modes of prediction the fourth seems to be most applicable to the state of the world at the moment. Mechanical projections of growth at constant rates either of population or of GNP, like those of Herman Kahn and Anthony Weiner,[1] are very dangerous and misleading in situations in which the cup of tea or the ecological niche is within sight of being filled. Today there is much evidence to suggest that humans, as a species, who have been expanding in what has also been an expanding niche for a half a million years, have almost certainly gotten to the point where the expansion of the niche on earth cannot go on for very long and where the filling of the niche seems to be in prospect in strictly historic time—time that certainly is measured in centuries, perhaps even in decades.[2] This is indeed a psychological, ecological, and economic crisis for the human race. In terms of their own evolution humans have been well adjusted to expansion for probably 100,000 years and very well adjusted to it for the last 10,000 years. The habits and institutions, and technologies and ideologies that have had survival value have been those well adapted to an age of expansion. Now that the age of expansion is coming to a close, a whole new set of ideas and institutions that have not previously adapted well to survival will become necessary for survival, and man's whole future depends on whether he can make this adjustment rapidly enough.

The niche is still, of course, expandable; the expansion of the human niche through increased knowledge has been one of the most striking features of human development. Natural resources are primarily a function of human knowledge, and even in the last 200 years we have probably been discovering new resources faster than we have been using up the old ones. How long this process can go on is a question that must be raised, even if it cannot be answered. It is clear that it cannot go on forever. However, we cannot predict knowledge; we do not know, for instance, whether nuclear fission power can be utilized effectively. We do not know what the limits are on the improved utilization of solar energy, and we do not know what improvements in the recycling of materials could be developed once we put our minds to it.

What is clear is that eventually we must face the "spaceship earth" and the classical stationary state when all the easily available geological capital of the earth will be used up, and we will have to fall back on a system of recycling materials from the oceans, the atmosphere, and the soils, primarily by the use of solar energy. We are still a very long way from this recycling technology, and we still do not know how many people the earth can support in this condition or what degree of comfort even the optimum population might attain. One thing is certainly becoming clear: that the poor two-thirds of the world population at the moment are quite unlikely to be able to achieve the standard of life of the rich countries within any foreseeable period in the future simply because of the absence of easily available power sources and materials. An image of the future that was fashionable even ten years ago was that of continually expanding population and per capita GNP all over the world. This image now seems to be increasingly unrealistic in the light of pollution, exhaustion, and the other ills of societies that are essentially living on their geological capital.

THE FUTURE OF THE GRANTS ECONOMY: THE "SOCIAL TRIANGLE"

Under these somewhat gloomy circumstances the problem of the future of the grants economy is of great interest and importance. We have seen that grants are composed of two elements—one arising out of the threat system (fear) and the other arising out of the integrative system (love). We cannot, therefore, accurately represent the relation between grants and exchange on a simple two-variable diagram. However, the social triangle is one way of showing these relationships (see Figure 8.1). Here we measure 100 percent threats at point T, 100 percent exchange at point E, and 100 percent integrative relation, or love, at point L. Any point bounded by the triangle then represents a combination of these proportions. Any point on the line TL would represent 100 percent grants economy.

There will be some boundary within the triangle, suggested by the dotted line, which encloses the feasible set of these three proportions. We

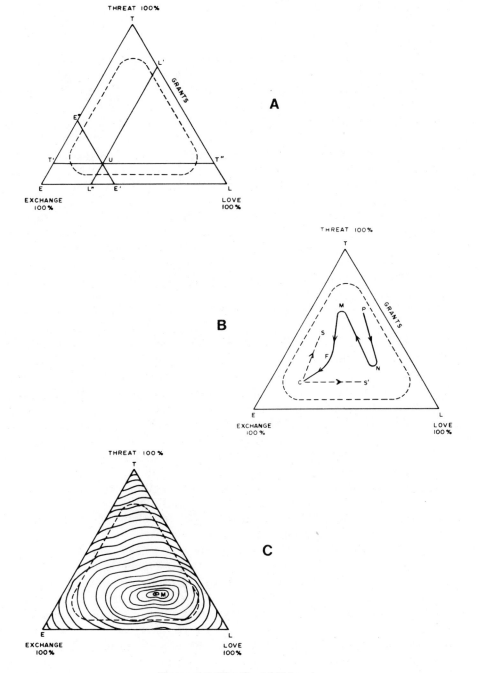

Figure 8.1 The Social Triangle

are supposing that no society can exist without at least some proportion of all three elements and that society is unlikely to exist where the proportion of any one is excessively high.

There are no accurate measures of these three proportions for any particular society. We could get a rough idea of the proportion of exchange to grants in the distribution of the product of total activity, which would at least locate the position on some line such as $E'E''$ within the triangle parallel to TL, but where on such a line we would make the division between threats and love is surprisingly difficult to determine. The amount of resources devoted to threat systems can be calculated with moderate accuracy, and this might well be a surrogate for a threat variable, in which case the integrative variable would be residual. Thus, in the United States if we allocate some 60 percent of the GNP to exchange and some 40 percent to grants, which seems to be about the figure if we include grants within the family, this would be represented by the line $E'E''$ in in Figure 8.1A, any point on which represents a combination of 60 percent exchange and 40 percent "threats and love" taken together. If we allocate 10 percent of the total to threat, representing the proportion of the GNP spent on the military and police, and the residual 30 percent on integrative relationships, we end up with a point such as U, which represents 60 percent exchange ($E'L$), 30 percent love (TL'), and 10 percent threat (ET').

In Figure 8.1B we represent in a rough kind of way the pattern of human history in the proportions of the three social organizers. There may be wide opportunity for disagreement about where a particular form of society would lie within the diagram, and the historical line $PNMFC$, as is actually drawn, must be regarded as highly tentative.[3] We start, however, at a point P in the paleolithic, at a high level of threat. This may just represent the conventional stereotype of the caveman with his club, and if we knew more about the societies of the paleolithic, we might put the point in a different place. The transition to the neolothic, N, however, undoubtedly represents a diminution of threat and an increase in the integrative system, as represented by religious and ritualistic institutions and the general absence of defense in the neolithic village. There is still not very much exchange, although no doubt some increase in metals, beads, pottery, and so on. The urban revolution and the rise of civilization and empires represents a shift to the point M at a much higher level of threat. Civilization is a product of the surplus food from agriculture plus the development of an organized threat system to take this surplus away from the food producer and with it feed soldiers, artisans, builders, priests, officials, and so on. As the empires succeed each other, there is a continual rise toward exchange as a merchant class develops and as mercantile cities develop independent of the political centers, leading toward the point F, which stands for the feudal system. This is at a somewhat higher level, both of exchange and of integrative mixture, than we have in the classical empires. Exchange increases in importance as we move toward C, which is capitalism, with a very high proportion of exchange and a relatively small reliance on either threats or integrative mechanisms. From C we have shown two possible paths, both leading toward a substantial diminution of the role of exchange. The one toward S is the movement toward totalitarianism, whether of the Right or of the Left—that is, toward an increase of threats and the substitution of threats for exchange. The one to S' would be toward a more democratic socialism, with exchange being replaced by integrative grants, arising out of a sense of community and identity with all members of the community.

A question of great interest, but one that cannot be answered without much further research, is, What is the ideal combination? Where within the social triangle is the optimum point? We could postulate, as in Figure 8.1C, a set of contours, the curved solid lines, of a goodness function in the third dimension above the paper, the point M being the top of the hill and representing the optimum point in the whole field and each of the contours representing an indifference curve—that is, all points in the field that have an equal value to the evaluator. As I have drawn the contours, we see a strong preference for the integrative section of society, although not so much that it would deny all value to exchange or even to threats. We see the secondary preference for exchange and a very low preference for threats. Other preferences would generate other patterns.

Another very interesting question is how far perceived divergences between the existing state of the system and the preferred state operate to change the system itself. How far, for instance, is the dynamic path of Figure 8.1C a result of changing opportunities rather than of changing preferences? This is a question again that cannot be answered with the present state of knowledge. It is, nevertheless, a key problem in the interpretation of history. How far, for instance, is the movement from the paleolithic into the neolothic a result of the invention of agriculture, with a consequent easing of human living and the development of a food surplus, which made integrative activities more rewarding and diminished the payoffs to threat? Up to a point this hypothesis certainly seems plausible. On the other hand, why was agriculture not invented earlier? One could argue on the other side that unless preferences had been developed for community life and for the sort of nurturing kind of feminine society that agriculture represents, agriculture would never have been invented, or if it had been invented, would not have survived in an aggressive, masculine-dominated caveman culture. Unfortunately, much of this process is lost in the mists of the past.

The movement from the neolithic into the civilized empires, and the so-called urban revolution of 3000 B.C., again may partly have been the result of the development of metallurgy with its improved weapons as well as improved agricultural implements. Cities—and after them, the empires—were a social invention in which charismatic leadership and religion seem to have played a prominent part. The first cities certainly seem to have been theocracies, which would put them closer to N on the line between N and M (Figure 8.1B). With the development of the habits of social organization, however, the role of the organized threat system arises, and the king or emperor, with his armies, relies much more on threat than on charisma and integrative networks. Moving from M toward F and C, again with the rise of exchange, may involve the development of certain integrative networks, such as religion, as an intermediary; they also may develop because the payoffs of exchange are much higher than the payoffs of the threat system. This is because of the famous principle of Adam Smith that the division of labor depends on the extent of the market; thus, trade promotes division of labor, which promotes productivity, which promotes further exchange, which promotes further productivity, and so on, in a process of "deviation amplifying positive feedback."[4]

GRANTS IN THE SPACESHIP EARTH

The instability of capitalism may arise partly out of certain technical defects of an elaborate exchange system that results in unemployment and depression; it also results from certain delegitimations of exchange, which may well arise because of strong preferences for integrative relationships, which are, after all, personally much more satisfying than exchange. To do things for love always seems to be more moral and progressive than to do things for money. So capitalism undermines itself, as Joseph Shumpeter pointed out, despite its success because of a failure of exchange institutions, such as finance, banking, corporations, and so on, to develop an integrative matrix that will legitimate them. Hence, we may get reversals, either to S or to S' (Figure 8.1B). Unfortunately, movements motivated toward S' often seem to end up at S (S perhaps stands for Joseph Stalin).

Certainly as knowledge grows and mankind becomes more aware of itself and its environment, we may expect that demand (the perception of divergence between the existing state of affairs and some state regarded as better or more ideal) is likely to play a larger role in the dynamics of society than the blind movements of technological evolution through mutation (invention) and selection. The dream of planning—that is, that humans could have an image of a preferred future toward which they would deliberately direct the movements of themselves and their society— is a dream that is perhaps not much more than 100 years old, but it nevertheless has caught the imagination of large numbers of people. Like all dreams, this one can easily turn into a nightmare, for the plan may turn out merely to be one more factor in an ecological evolutionary situation over which we have no real control, and because we have the plan, we may end up worse off than we otherwise would have been. In Figure 8.1B, shall we say, from C we plan to go to S', which is a preferred position, but because of the existence of the plan we actually end up at S, which is actually worse off than we were before. The history of revolutions and of planned economies is by no means encouraging in this regard.

The fact that some plans may be worse than no plan does not rule out the possibility that there are other plans that would be better than no plan. The search for these better plans seems to be almost inevitable with the rise of social self-consciousness. Planning, indeed, is almost part of the price we pay for consciousness. We can hardly have consciousness without directing our energies toward some conscious image of the future. It is a curious irony that it is just at the moment when consious images of the future become important in the dynamics of society that the future takes on this closed claustrophobic quality of movement toward the spaceship earth and a stationary state from which there seems to be little chance of escape.

The critical question for the human race today, therefore, is, How can we make the best of what may be quite a bad job and move toward that organization of world society that will make the spaceship earth tolerable? The notion that we are moving into an era of vast abundance and leisure thanks to the wonders of science, computers, and automation that was popular even a few years ago does now seem to be an illusion. However, there is nothing in the social sciences that says that a reasonably comfortable, decent, warm, charitable, well-managed, and creative society would be impossible in a spaceship earth. What is clear is that it will be difficult, that the achievement of a society compatible with the human race's evolutionary potential is not something that will come automatically of itself but something that will demand an intellectual and moral effort of an intensity of which the human race is undoubtedly capable but has not yet achieved.

Furthermore, the road that leads toward the spaceship earth is beset with frightful dangers and difficulties. We do not know, for example, what population a spaceship earth can support in a stable, high-level economy because this knowledge depends on a knowledge and technology still to come. The most pessimistic view is that present high-level economies are based on the spendthrift use of geological capital and that the present expansion of world population is a result of this. Once the capital is gone we must face a drastic reduction of the human population if we are not to fall back into desperate poverty. This has never been accomplished in human history, at any rate, without catastrophe and agonizing human suffering. The feeling that we may be living in a golden age is a very uncomfortable, bittersweet emotion.

On the other hand, the pessimistic view is not necessarily justified. It may be that the spaceship earth, with new knowledge of the efficient utilization of solar energy and of the recycling of materials, could sustain in comfort and decency the 4 billion crew that it now has, or even the 8 billion it may have before any population increase can be curbed, in which case the transition to the spaceship earth might be achieved without massive catastrophe or human suffering. We need a major intellectual effort at the moment in the physical sciences, in engineering, in biology, in the social sciences, and in philosophical, political, and religious thought to discover and to work toward the conditions under which the optimistic solution may be feasible. If it turns out not to be feasible, then we must learn how to survive the agony of transition without permitting the processes of survival to destroy the hope of a decent world.

These may seem like very large considerations for a book that is primarily concerned with a rather technical point of the social sciences. Nevertheless, I believe that the problem of the relative role of grants and exchange in the world of the future is one of the most crucial elements in determining the nature of the movement toward the spaceship earth and even in determining the possibility of attaining it. My own values incline me strongly toward a society in which grants, and especially reciprocity, play an important role; in which the sense of community is strong but also in which the community encourages individuality and freedom, opportunity for variety and divergences, and other values that can only be fostered in an exchange matrix. We must find the proper proportions and proper use of all three social organizers if this desperate and precarious dynamic path toward the spaceship earth, beset as it is with frightful precipices, is to be walked safely. If there is a political message from this work, the message is that no existing ideology, developed as they all have been in a dynamic and expanding human race, is in any way adequate to deal with the problems of the future. The theory of the grants economy is a humble and unpretentious foundation for the ideology to come. I believe that without this foundation the ideology that will guide us through the future cannot be built.

NOTES

1. Herman Kahn and Anthony J. Wiener, *The Year 2000* (New York: Macmillan, 1967).
2. See Donella H. Meadows, Dennis L. Meadows, Jørgen Randers, and William W. Behrens III, *The Limits to Growth* (New York: Universe Books, 1972); Jay W. Forrester, *World Dynamics* (Cambridge, Mass.: Wright-Allen Press, 1971); Ronald D. Ridker and William O. Watson, *To Choose a Future* (Baltimore and London: Johns Hopkins University Press, for

Resources for the Future, 1980); *The Global 2000 Report to the President* (Washington, D.C.: U.S. Government Printing Office, 1980).

3. I am indebted to Dr. Joseph F. Follettie, of the Southwest Regional Laboratory for Educational Research and Development, for the idea of this construction, although he should not be blamed for this particular application.

4. See M. Maruyama, "The Second Cybernetics: Deviation Amplifying Mutual Causal Processes," *American Scientist* 51 (1963): 164–79.

Index

About the Author

KENNETH E. BOULDING is Distinguished Professor of Economics Emeritus and Director, Program on General Social and Economic Dynamics at the Institute of Behavioral Science, The University of Colorado in Boulder.

He is a past president of the American Economic Association, the International Studies Association, and the American Association for the Advancement of Science, and is currently president of the Association for the Study of the Grants Economy.

He is the author of some 25 books. His Collected Papers have been issued in five volumes. He is a member of the National Academy of Sciences, the American Academy of Arts and Sciences, and the American Philosophical Association.

Born in Liverpool, England, in 1910, he has lived in the United States since 1937, and has taught at Colgate University, Fisk University, Iowa State College, and the University of Michigan before coming to Colorado in 1967. He has held visiting professorships and lectureships around the world. He was a founder and the first president of the Society for General Systems Research. His most recent works include Ecodynamics, a New Theory of Societal Evolution; Stable Peace; and Evolutionary Economics.